ANIMATED EDIBLEZ

Feisty Vegetables and Incredible Starches

∽∞∽

Vee Ward

*To Michael
Enjoy!!!
Vee*

Copyright © 2012 by Vee Ward
All rights reserved.

ISBN: 1466497254
EAN-13: 9781466497252

Serving good food is a perfect expression of love.

This series of books is dedicated to my children Yvette, Derek, Michael and Robbie; my brother Bernard, now deceased, who thought it was his appointed duty, to always with humor, critique my culinary skills; my parents Margarette and Charles; Rene my initial editor; my husband Ed; Aunt Flo; and my Gourmet Sisters Club members. All of whom gave me endless encouragement to write this cookbook.

By Vee Ward
The Animated Gourmet

Cover by Truentity
truentity1@yahoo.com

Forward

Vee Ward has a real winner here! Nobody expects to be entertained by a cookbook, yet you'll find yourself unable to stop turning the pages of this unusual, quirky and very uplifting kitchen gem. In addition to some wonderful recipes and great tips, you'll find an abundance of humor and joy between these pages — both of which are greatly needed in our world today. Thank you Vee Ward for bringing a sense of fun back into the home.

— R.D. Nelson
Author of MEINONG'S JUNGLE

ANIMATED EDIBLEZ
FEISTY VEGETABLES AND INCREDIBLE STARCHES

INTRODUCTION

FIRST BOOK OF THE SERIES*

"Animated Ediblez" is a non-traditional cookbook that offers cooks of all ages uncomplicated recipes, humorous conversations, and historical snippets seasoned with tales of laugh out loud kitchen escapades.

"Feisty Vegetables and Incredible Starches" is the first of a planned three-part set of cookbooks sprinkled with money saving tips, buying guides, secrets to making the best food purchases and nutritional information. Aspiring cooks will learn how to spice up their everyday dishes by simply adding one or two ingredients to offer a change the entire family will enjoy.

Readers of "Animated Ediblez" will find this unique cookbook a wildly new kind of novella that will elicit much laughter from the author's conversations with food.

"Animated Ediblez" has created a new niche of cookbooks focusing on staples such as potatoes, carrots, and tomatoes that have been smashed, cut into various sizes and shapes, had nutritional benefits cooked out of them, and thrown on the dinner table like discarded nutshells. This cookbook explores new and exciting recipes for these staples and introduces many neglected vegetables into budget meals.

Readers will learn to demystify the complexities of common cooking failures and bond with entertaining veggie and starch characters.

A *"Tell All Section"* in the appendix is a quick reference guide to cookbook jargon, and cooking utensil information. An asterisk in a recipe indicates an explanation can be found in the "Tell All Section".

* Super Star Meats and Gregarious Seafood;
Cutesy Appetizers and Desserts for Suga' Lovers.

TABLE OF CONTENTS

A Peek at the Author   1
The Art of Being Creative   2
Freshness Tips and More   3
What Would Grandma Say?   3
Origin, Bruising and Butter   4
Industry Secrets   4

VEGETABLE STORIES   7

Tomatoes   9
Carrots   13
Onions   17
Garlic   21
Leeks   25
Shallots/Scallions   27
Down Home Greens   29
Cabbage   33
Bok Choy   35

Cauliflower   39
Kohlrabi   41
Brussels Sprouts   43
Asparagus   45
Green Beans & Associates   49
Fresh Lima Beans   53
Eggplant   57
Squash   59
Spaghetti Squash   65

Rutabaga, Parsnips & Turnips   69

Maize/Corn   73

Exotic Mushrooms   77

Portabello Mushrooms   81

Sugar Beets, Anyone   85

STARCH STORIES   87

Pasta   89

Noodles   89

Centuries of Rice   93

White Potato, Gold Potato, Red Potato   97

VEGETABLE RECIPES   101

Fantastic Stewed Tomatoes   103

Michael's Yummy Carrot Casserole   105

Best Dang Hot or Cold Carrot Salad   106

Positively Smashing Smothered Onions   107

Margaret's Spicy Garlic Pepper Sauce   108

Must Have Roasted Garlic Paste   109

Sugar and Spice Leeks and Broccoli   110

Stir Fry Scallion Topper   111

Delectable Creamed Shallots and Spinach   112

Nora's Cauliflower Smush   113

Cauliflower and Friends   114

Mr. Ed's World Famous Cabbage   115

Liz's Fried Cabbage   116

Stick to the Ribs Mixed Greens   117

Collards and Cabbage   118

Mmmm Good Vegetarian Stir Fry   119

Jump 'n and Dancin' Roasted Kohlrabi   120

Sautéed Kohlrabi   121

Plainly Speaking Brussels Sprouts   122

Dressed Up Brussels Sprouts   123

Yvette's Sophisticated Asparagus   124

Asparagus in Lemon Juice   125

Green Beans Kozy   126

Steamed Green Beans Almondine   127

Tantalizing Green Lima Beans   128

Denise's Succotash with Pazzz   129

French Fried Eggplant Stiks   130

Zipping Hot Stuffed Grilled Eggplant   131

Yellow Squash & Zucchini Combo   132

Derek's Baked Yellow Squash   133

Spectacular Batter Fried Squash Flowers   134

Muriel's Spaghetti Squash Casserole   135

Winky's Mashed Rutabaga   136

Roasted Parsnips and Turnips   137

Good to the Last Kernel Corn Pudding   138

Dorothy's Fried Corn   139

Old South Corn Fritters   140

Euronne's Sautéed Oychanshi* Mushroom Surprise   141

Robbie's Mushroom and Onion Delight   142

Tia's Portobellos Italiano   143

Portobello Burgers Whiz   144

Silky Sweet Beets   145

Roasted Beets   146

Wacky Onion Beets   147

STARCH RECIPES 149

Some Kind of Good Rice   153

Baked Cheesy Rice and Onion Pie   154

Calvin's Dirty Rice and Tomato Casserole   155

Good Ole Red Beans and Rice   156

Aunt Flo's Spinach and Bermuda Onion Risotto   157

Italian Veggie Pasta   161

Craig's Feel Good Linguini Alfredo   162

World's Best Macaroni and Cheese   163

Grandpa's Spaghetti and Meat Sauce   164

Spaghetti and Parmesan Nests   165

Baked Egg Noodles   169

Noodle Veggie Soup   170

Kick 'n Potatoes au Gratin   173

Southern Home Fries   174

Elegant Mashed Potatoes   175

Miz Margarette's Twice Baked Potatoes   176

Come 'n Get 'em Roasted Red Potatoes   177

Rich and Sassy Cold Potato Soup (Vichyssoise)   178

Simply Simple Fingerling Potatoes   179

Kel's Mouthwatering Sweet Potatoes   180

Connie's Fluffy Baked Sweet Potatoes   182

Richard's Grits and Sausage Bake   183

TELL ALL SECTION 185

PREFERENCES   187
RESOURCES   189

A Peek at the Author

For as long as I can remember, I've had a love affair with food. Some people dream of making money; I dream of preparing delightful, well-crafted meals. Entertaining and witty conversations with food spurs me on to transcend the limits of ordinary creativity.

My experience with food is a compilation of learning to cook at age seven under my mother's watchful eye. As I grew older and more experienced my cooking roles expanded to wife, mother, caterer, and finally an *Animated Gourmet*. What is that you ask? I have defined the term as *diddling* with the ingredients and finding *humor* while doing it. I am not a cooking expert I just want to bring fun and laughter to the kitchen.

Give it a try! Explore the concept of humor while twirling around in the kitchen. Come on, engage in verbal combat and silliness with food—it will appear to shorten your time in the most dreaded room in your house…the kitchen. Conversing with food can make you a star in the eyes of your adoring public. Well, at least in the eyes of your family and friends.

One important note: I have discovered that some foods *do not* have a gift for gab; some are hesitant while others have just plain ignored me.

Just the other day I put too much Thai pepper sauce in the potato salad I was making and immediately reprimanded myself aloud, "Have you lost your mind, how are you going to fix this?" The salad ingredients responded with a blare of hot breath that made my eyes water "Add more potatoes, Silly." I did and another mistake was rescued from the garbage heap.

The Art of Being Creative

Feeding the eye as well as the stomach is as essential as clean plates. Visualize a beautifully set table with all of the accoutrements for a gastronomical feast. With a few lessons, you too can create such a masterpiece. Let your creative juices flow and watch your budget meals take on a life of their own. All that it takes is a smidgen of desire to expand your veggie horizons, and a veggie to plan around. Then open the door to your imagination, reach inside and unlock the trunk that is holding your creativity hostage.

In one of my spurts of creativity I sprinkled a spoonful of poultry seasoning and a smattering of butter on green peas to entice my son to eat them. He loved them.

Experiment. Set aside small portions of food and have at it. If your idea doesn't work, who's to know? Many of my experiments have been fodder for the garbage disposal.

Special occasions create opportunities to put a new spin on everyday foods and gives rise to exploration of unusual ingredients such as quail eggs as a topper on appetizers.

Introduce new and revamped vegetables to your table gradually. It can be an awesome experience, especially when your family and friends "ooh" and "ahh" while lavishing accolades on you. Cooking can also be good therapy when you've had a bad day. *Beat that cake batter, chop that celery*; see, you feel better already.

Freshness Tips and More

Fresh veggies should be purchased, most importantly for their nutritional benefits. Freshness dates are not printed on vegetables, so I suggest that fresh vegetables be selected with care, especially in these times of tight money. Purchasing vegetables in bulk is only practical when they are to be frozen for future use and the price is acceptable to your budget. Prolonging preparation is a waste of money and results in decreased nutritional value of your produce.

Prior to freezing veggies must be blanched. This easy process consists of plopping them in boiling water for no more than ten minutes. Drain and cover with cold water. Throw them into plastic bags indicating the contents and the date. Do not freeze cabbage or asparagus. They become inedible. Onions, celery and peppers do not require blanching, chop and bag for freezing.

What Would Grandma Say?

Once you have mastered a recipe by adding or substituting ingredients, share it with others. Back in the day, cooks would say, "This is Grandma's secret recipe and she wouldn't want me to share it with anyone." When you share your jewel of a recipe you and grandma can claim creative genius status. Wherever she is she will say, "Hot diggety, instant fame." If you have updated Grandma's recipe to appeal to today's palates add that to your spiel when accepting kudos for it. Soon you and grandma will become food gurus, whatever that is.

Origin, Bruising and Butter (OBB)

O   Knowing the origin of a food can spice up a recipe and be an indicator of other indigenous ingredients to that growing area. Many food preparation questions can be answered by locating the origin of the food and a bit of food history.

B   Typically, most thin-skinned vegetables will have some bruising. That's okay, but extensive bruising is not. Bruising is due mostly to rough handling of crates during transport.

B   I prefer butter in my recipes, but feel free to substitute any fat that appeals to your taste buds and health issues. For me, butter is the best flavor enhancer.

Today, most health conscious cooks prefer olive oil. Olive oil varieties are extensive and include extra light for salads, extra virgin for most preparations, cold pressed, Italian, Spanish, Greek...you get the picture. Each lends a special flavor to recipes from those areas of the world.

Most cooks use vegetable oil in their recipes. However, from the dark ages through the fifties solid shortening and lard were the most prominent fats on the market. Lard, although hard on the arteries makes the best pie crust and refried beans.

Little Known Fact: The lowly peanut produces great frying oil, but did you know that it is not a nut at all but a vegetable, as are cantaloupe and watermelon. Surprise! Surprise!

Industry Secrets

Agonizing over your food because it doesn't look like the picture in the magazine? I will share some food styling tricks I recently discovered: Most foods are undercooked, painted with food dye or some such stuff to make them appear irresistible. Here are a few helpful ideas to get you started...to get that glossy look on vegetables pour a little melted butter over them.

For bread and pie crust that shimmers brush on an egg wash (one beaten egg and a bit of water) before baking, or rub a stick of butter over the top after baking.

The following process will make your meats glisten like new money. Remove meat from baking pan. In a small bowl add a few spoonfuls of the drippings to cornstarch this will make a smooth thin paste. Heat drippings on top of the stove; gradually stir in cornstarch mixture until drippings are slightly thickened. Brush over meat before serving. Your guests will marvel at the sight. This idea can be used successfully with most meats and poultry.

Now it's time to get a bottle of water, a glass of juice, or perhaps a cocktail, and settle into your favorite chair, or wherever you feel comfy, and prepare to enjoy the rest of the book.

Ready? Let's get started!

VEGETABLE STORIES

TOMATOES

This beautiful red fruit has been around for thousands of years. Today, tomatoes come to us not only in shades of red, but also in yellow, green, pink, purple, and cream, and are loaded with Lycopene and other antioxidants. How good is that! There are so many varieties that it would be impossible to speak about them all. Tomato varieties range from ABC Potato Leaf to Zuckertraube. Here are a few I found notable: Fuzzy Cherokee (purple), Roman Candle (yellow), and Rugby (orange).

The most popular tomatoes today are the heirlooms, which include over one hundred varieties. The cutest tomato shape is the Grightmires Pride, a tomato that resembles a raindrop. The most unusual name, in my opinion, is the Jujube Cherry. Too much information? Oh, well, at least you are prepared to win at Jeopardy.

TOMATO TRIVIA

Tomatoes grow in almost every country and have no shortage of uses. Because people often refer to their loved ones as fruits or vegetables, this piece of history is important. The tomato is sometimes referred to as a "love apple" or "wolf peach." At other times, as a "yellow apple," "Hello, my Yellow Apple" isn't nearly as romantic as saying to your beloved, "Come here my Wolf Peach," who then responds "Coming, my Love Apple."

In 1893, the U.S. Supreme Court ruled that tomatoes be considered a vegetable, even though, botanically, they are a fruit. The ruling to categorize tomatoes was necessary due to import taxes. The mandate reduced disputes over which tax to impose on imported tomatoes.

OH, MY, OH, MY WHICH ONES TO BUY?

Some tomatoes are sweet as honey while others are tangy and sour. Nearly all will appeal to your taste buds when used in recipes with ingredients that enhance their flavor. I prefer to buy loose tomatoes sold by the pound for better overall quality.

Of the many varieties of tomatoes, I will share my secret for which ones make the best fresh stewed tomato dish. I use those not-so appealing nor flavorful hothouse tomatoes—the ones on the display cube looking blasé. I was amazed when they told me to pair them with plum tomatoes—together they make a sensational duo and stretch the dollar. Hurray for plain and unappetizing.

Save vine-ripened tomatoes, those with the vine attached, for salads. They are too good for cooking, unless—and there is always an unless—the flavor required for a dish will be greatly enhanced by these wunderkinds.

"Ordinaries" is what I call hothouse tomatoes. Being rather tasteless, they are usually the most reticent. These tomatoes have sense enough to know when not to speak. Fortunately for me, the ordinaries I encountered one day long ago had a lot to say.

"Excuse me Miss. Excuse me."

I looked quizzically over my shoulder at Old Smiley Face and replied, "Yes?"

"Known for being ordinary, we would like you to hook up

with us and our buddies over there," he said, motioning toward the plum tomatoes. "We will help you create a scrumptious dish."

Teasing them I said, "Why would I want to do that?"

"Begging your pardon Miss, let's do a little rocking and rolling. We are here to rock your world, and you will roll with the information."

Just then, another tomato near the top of the heap broke out in a raucous tune. Abruptly, I ended its performance with, "Okay, buster, you and your mates climb into this plastic bag. *Now!*"

"Not without our friends, the plums. Remember, together we are a dynamic duo."

"Alright, already," I said impatiently while holding two plastic bags for them to wobble into.

In my newly renovated kitchen, I began looking through a cookbook for recipes to humor my latest houseguests, but without much success. Old Smiley Face brought me back into the moment with, "Whew, that was a long ride to your kitchen counter."

"Well, you're here now, so let's get it on." I said.

I turned the TV to a music channel, pulled out my cutting board from the drawer under the sink, and then reached for the sharpest knife in the block. My plan was to whack them good. Blade hovering over an ordinary tomato's top, I stopped in midair when I heard "Wait, wait." The tomato wiggled out from under the shadow of the knife blade in an effort to humor me and said, "Before you mangle us let me give you a recipe extraordinaire."

I reconsidered my course of action and thought that I might as well listen to what my loquacious buddy had to say. Heck, I had spent eight dollars on these buggers. So, with open ears and a tight grip on my knife I prepared the recipe as instructed.

BUYING GUIDE: Purchase only firm to the touch tomatoes, never those that can be passed off as rocks unless (here we go again) you plan to use them in slow cooking recipes. Generally, these rocks have a tangy flavor. Purchase only as many tomatoes as can be used within two or three days.

STORAGE: To retain the flavor of tomatoes, do not refrigerate them, especially those you plan to use for salads. However, do keep them in a cool place. If you must refrigerate tomatoes, allow them to return to room temperature before serving.

CARROTS
Best of the Lollipop Veggies

Do you know that carrots are a taproot vegetable? Taproot veggies grow downward in the soil. See, you learned something new right away.

MYTHICAL USES

I haven't a clue why Caligula, and many other Romans of his era, thought that veggies had aphrodisiacal properties. They believed that they would produce a more virile male and a more willing female. I eat them all the time and serve them to the husband—nothing.

Another myth has been floating around since time began that carrots improve eyesight. According to one World War II Air Force unit, it may be true. The pilots bragged that their accuracy was due to eating large quantities of carrots. Whatever floats your boat!

HISTORICAL SNIPPET

Carrots started out as a refined weed, "Queen Ann's Lace" and due to over-zealous horticulturalists grew into many sizes, shapes, and colors. In Holland, someone with a sense of humor decided to hybridize the red, purple, black, yellow, and white varieties, and voilà orange carrots were born. WOW! What a genius.

Loaded with beta carotene, sweet carrot juice is a welcome ingredient in smoothies and, thanks to the colonists, we in the New World can enjoy carrots as a healthy portable snack. Raw carrots are nutritionally good, but according to the latest reports, cooked carrots are even better. Supposedly, cooking releases the nutrients. What a revelation!

MY LESSON

Out of nowhere came an intellectual sounding voice, "Our common color is O R A N G E, however we segue into white or a red-white blend."

"So!"

The voice responded, "Dear Lady, I have so much to offer to a healthy diet. I retain my beautiful full flavor and color regardless of what you do to me."

"Alright, friend, tell me what you can do other than crunch when eaten raw or recline limp in a bowl when cooked."

"No, no, no! Why such a poor image of us? You're in for a surprise! We will take you from an average carrot preparer to a star in your own kitchen."

"And just how do you propose to do that?"

"The only way you will find out is to take a bunch of us home with you."

Reluctantly, I searched for and found the best-looking bunch on the display cube.

At home, I began preparing lunch with no thought of the carrots resting in the plastic bag in the sink.

"Hey! Down here." The words penetrated my thoughts. The voice came at me again. "Remember our promise? Get a pen and paper Missy."

I looked in my catchall drawer for a pad and pen. With pen poised over the paper, the intellectual carrot and I began an endearing friendship.

BUYING GUIDE: *Do Not* purchase namby, pamby* carrots. Carrots should be hard and have few growth spots. *Growth spots are root indentations.* I have seen carrots as hairy as a kitten; not good. These hairs are roots and a sign that the carrots have stayed in the ground or somewhere else too long.

Today, baby carrots are all the rage. However, it is interesting to note that all of those nubby carrots are not actually baby carrots as is often advertised; they are big carrots cut to resemble baby carrots. *Read the label.*

STORAGE: All full-sized refrigerators have vegetable storage bins, some with climate control. With or without climate control, you can store carrots at the bottom of the bin with other vegetables. Carrots' longevity allows you to place them under vegetables with a shorter freshness span. *Do not* allow carrots to grow those cute little flowers on their tops again, they cause deterioration of nutrients.

ONIONS

ORIGINS AND MYTHICAL USES

Although, onions have been cultivated for thousands of years, their country of origin is still a mystery. Wild onions were probably a favorite of cavemen. Can you imagine a caveman with onion breath warding off a tyrannosaurus? Now that would have been a Kodak® moment.

In 1160 BCE old King Ramses IV died and his embalmers placed onions in his eye sockets. Perhaps they believed the onions would restore his sight in the next world or after a long and arduous journey, he would be hungry and would at least have the onions to eat. Ooo, what an unpleasant thought.

Thirsty? Eat an onion. Food is short and you are hungry? Make onion soup. Onions are said to have medicinal and magical properties. Medicinal? Okay, that's possible, but magical? Maybe in the Twilight Zone®.

HISTORICAL SNIPPETS

History tells us that onions are exceptionally versatile. They can be eaten fried, sautéed, raw, baked, grilled, broiled, and boiled. Whew! That was a mouthful. They also have the distinction of complementing many other vegetables, meats, and salads. Cooks use them more as an addition to a dish rather than a stand-alone veggie.

Prior to the most popular onions currently on the market—the imported Chilean sweet ones—were the Georgia grown Vidalias, and recently the famous and expensive Maui varieties. They are oh, soooo good. When frying these onions, there is no need to add water to simmer; they produce just enough liquid to complete the job. Their sweet flesh is tantalizing. Especially if you feel steak isn't steak without onions, or liver is incomplete without them.

Moving on! Yellow onions are a universal favorite. There isn't anything you can't do with the yellow guys. Baked, they lose their strong flavor and become docile. Frying adds a slightly sweet taste when you add a little water. And raw, oh my, you can't beat a bowl of hot chili with a heaping spoonful of chopped raw yellow onions to satisfy a hunger for their sharp flavor.

The red or Bermuda onions are, in my humble opinion, best served raw. Their dark red hue adds color, their flavor perks up salads, and they are quite decorative. Pearl onions are the "cutie pies," and so easy to prepare. Today's onions aren't often the *tearjerkers* they used to be. Occasionally, a yellow onion will make me a little weepy but on the whole onions today are more flavorful and less menacing.

Recently, I discovered two great varieties. Cipolline onions—tiny donut-shaped wonders—have a very strong odor but are quite tasty. Banana onions are the ones to use to impress guests. Peeled and sautéed whole in butter, they take their place alongside the most elegantly prepared veggies.

MY ENCOUNTER

I was like a child in a candy store all aglow as I gazed at the organic vegetables in a famous super market. There were vegetables there that I had only seen on TV, banana onions among them. I trembled with ecstasy at the thought of serving these gems to my gourmet club members.

Gently, I touched one with my forefinger. Then I picked it up and sniffed it. My eyes drifted to the sign above them. It read, "Banana Onions $5 per pound." I went all fuzzy inside. Even if I bought two per person, they would probably weigh no more than a pound. Who cares, I thought, I am giving them the meal of a lifetime.

Suddenly it dawned on me there weren't any recipe cards in the rack to help me in my quest to impress my guests. Undaunted, I purchased my wonderful treat and sped down the highway. On the ride home, I began to worry, what if I spoil them? I'm sure that is a thought all cooks can relate to.

In my kitchen, I searched for recipes from among the myriad of cookbooks I have. Nothing! Then my creative juices began to flow. First, I should see what the new kids on the block had to say.

I stroked one of the onions and it cooed as if it were a baby.

In a soothing voice I said, "Tell me the secret to successful preparation of your delicate little bodies."

The onions lay there on the counter like pet rocks. Tears began forming in my eyes. I begged, "Please give me your secret."

"Calm down, Madame."

I was so excited to hear them speak. I picked up the little fellow closest to my trembling hand and kissed it.

"Sautéing us whole in butter enhances our flavor. Remember now, keep us whole. If you wish, you can add fresh mushrooms to our juices while sautéing."

"I can't thank you enough. Thank you, thank you." I gushed.

On the day of the dinner, as I plated my beautiful Banana onions, I heard a couple that I hadn't used say, "Madame, you have done us proud."

My Club members delighted in their succulent flavor and praised my culinary skills once again.

BUYING GUIDE: Firm onions are a must for flavor and nutrients. Beware of onions in bags, as they sometimes contain one or two that are on the edge of spoiling. Examine all of the onions in the bag for freshness. *Do not* buy onions with stems growing out of their tops they are ready for the garbage pail.

STORAGE: Remove the plastic bag. Dump onions in a separate bin or with potatoes. Gases from these little buggers can cause other vegetables to spoil. If there isn't enough room in the refrigerator for separation, store them elsewhere in a cool, dry, dark place. Quickly use onions that are shedding their outer skin.

GARLIC

Garlic. Oh, yes, yes, yes! I love those smelly little bulbs. Garlic is a favorite of cooks on every continent. No Italian or Chinese meal would be complete without a handful of chopped garlic. And besides, it was once thought that garlic also had aphrodisiacal properties. Probably accounts for yesteryear's large families.

GARLIC TRIVIA

A native of Central Asia, the popularity of this much-maligned staple has come into its own around the world. Hippocrates perpetuated the myth that garlic should be used for infections, wounds, and intestinal disorders, and if that failed, they should be used in a good lamb stew.

Those misguided Roman soldiers—egotistical war mongers that they were—attributed their strength, courage, and stamina to this wee bulb.

Hanging garlic is discouraged unless, of course, you live in Transylvania in which case, hang some over your doors and windows to ward off vampires. A tip to all Transylvanian men: instead of a flower in your lapel, I have heard that a sprig of garlic can do wonders for your sex life. Transylvanian ladies, with the shortage of eligible men you may not want to adorn yourself with garlic sprigs in case a handsome vampire is your last chance at love.

HISTORY OF THE WEE BULB

There are ten groups of garlic that espouse several varieties. Garlic arrived in America with the Polish, German, and Italian immigrants. Today, Gilroy, California is the garlic Capital of the World. No kidding! They even have a festival every year to benefit local charities. Garlic festivals are held worldwide. A few well know festivals are held in the Hudson Valley in New York, in Perth Ontario, Canada, and on the Isle of Wight in England.

Although notorious for its pungency and for giving us bad breath, this bulb has for thousands of years has been known for its effective medicinal properties on those of us who suffer with high cholesterol and hypertension.

Beware! Elephant garlic is not garlic at all. It is a fabulous Egyptian leek. It does, however, give dishes the same flavor as real garlic, just not as strong. Garlic is used in bread and soups, and mixed with other veggies. It is also pushed into meats, and made into paste for sauces and dips. Famous garlic dishes include garlic bread, garlic mashed potatoes and garlic shrimp (scampi.)

To remove the skin from fresh garlic, pound the clove with the flat side of a wide blade knife and it will come apart easily. Use the same process for elephant garlic.

GARLIC SPEAKS WITHOUT SAYING A WORD

Garlic is very reticent. It only speaks to our taste buds. And boy did it speak to mine.

My taste buds were in the mood for something different, something highly pungent. Why? My husband had committed the ultimate sin. He said within earshot of our guests that he was not pleased with the sweet potato casserole I had prepared.

Nodding to him to follow me into the kitchen I expressed my uncertainty of his remark, since he had not tasted it.

He said rather matter-of-factly, "My mother made sweet potato casserole in a square pan."

I responded quizzically, "So?"

"I'm sure yours won't taste the same because it isn't in a square pan."

My fury was about to be unleashed; instead, I controlled myself and decided upon a better course of action. Every day for a week I ate two whole heads of roasted garlic. Yum! The consequences for him? My garlic breath became his constant nighttime companion. That week my husband learned a valuable lesson: Never criticize the cook you sleep with.

BUYING GUIDE: Garlic can be purchased in sleeves of ten or more. Unless you use huge quantities frequently, this is a waste of money. The exception: Fantastic Roasted Garlic Paste (see recipe). The rule of thumb is two to four cloves of garlic per recipe, more if you like sleeping on the sofa. Garlic is sometimes sold for ninety-nine cents per pound, which may seem expensive but the average head of garlic only weighs a few ounces, so go for it. Examine each head of garlic to ensure firm fresh cloves. If the garlic's papery outer skin collapses under gentle pressure, it is an indication the head has stayed too long at the party.

STORAGE: To prolong the life of garlic, regular or elephant, store it in the refrigerator with the onions.

LEEKS

Leeks have been enjoyed since ancient Egyptians began their pyramid projects. A member of the onion family, the flavor of leeks is subtle and sweet. Leeks don't speak. But they sure can turn potato soup, stir-fry, and roasts into a spectacular feast.

WARRING AND SINGING

Want to win a war? Beginning with King Cadwallader of Wales, Welsh soldiers wore leeks in their hats to distinguish them from their enemies. And guess what? They won the war between the Welsh and the Saxons. Today, they wear leek patches as an emblem of pride.

Nut job, Nero, ate leeks to improve his singing voice. What a waste of good leeks, he still screeched.

IMPORTANT TIPS

The white bulb is the edible part; the green tops are usually discarded or used as a garnish. Rinse leeks thoroughly—remnants of soil tend to linger inside the bulb. Try leeks in a stir-fry. Good, good, good!

BUYING GUIDE: The bulbs should be firm and as unblemished as possible. The green tops, although usually discarded, should also be firm. Purchase small to medium bulbs.

STORAGE: Removing the tops will not affect the flavor of the bulb during storage. Wrap leeks in foil to prolong their freshness. Store leeks with onions and garlic in the vegetable bin.

SHALLOTS/SCALLIONS
Gourmet Members of the Onion Family

HISTORY IN A SHALLOT SHELL

This gentle bulb made its presence known as early as 300 BCE. Shallots and scallions are interrelated, mild-flavored forms of onions that made them popular with the Patrician crowd in Rome. Those finicky eaters ate them raw and pickled.

True shallot bulbs come in an abundance of shapes, colors, and sizes. Best known are the golden brownish-skinned shallots. Many varieties are sold only in specialty markets.

Today we eat them boiled, fried, pickled, grilled, raw, and any other way our imagination leads us to prepare them. Use shallots in any recipe that calls for onions.

Green onions are often referred to as scallions. Those beautiful green tops are a great substitute for chives. Green onion tops are loaded with vitamins A, C, a few other nutritious tidbits, and sugar, sugar, sugar. Just thought I would throw that in.

SPEAK TO ME SHALLOTS...OR NOT

Shallots and scallions are so popular that their reputation speaks for them. And, they speak volumes to our taste buds. I like to use shallots in single servings of tuna salad—saves money. Although, these tiny wonders haven't spoken to me, they have expressed their happiness by never failing to sparkle in my recipes and as exquisite garnish.

BUYING GUIDE: Test the freshness of shallots and scallions by gently applying pressure to the bulb: no give, no problem. Unless large appeals to you, only buy small scallions. Buy green onion bulbs with erect green tops. Just because they are advertised three bunches for whatever price, buy only as many as you can use quickly.

STORAGE: By now you know the procedure for storing. Yes, with the rest of the family. Wrap in foil to prolong the freshness of scallions. Shallots may be stored loose with the onions.

DOWN HOME GREENS
Kale, Collards, Turnip, Rape, and Mustard Greens

GREENS, GREENS AND MORE GREENS

Collard greens, akin to kale, are among the oldest members of the cabbage family, dating back to prehistoric times. The Greeks enjoyed a good mess of collard greens and kale mixed together.

Some long ago historian said that the Romans introduced collards and kale to England, France, and Ireland. Well, in their quest for world domination, that is believable.

Prepared southern style, collard, turnip, rape, and mustard greens make delicious and nutritious side dishes. Cooking greens down to the lowest terms produces *pot likker*, a vitamin enriched broth that is usually thrown out. But, try some on corn bread, um, um good.

Little Known Fact: Ground rapeseed is the key ingredient in Dijon mustard.

BELLY WARMING ORIGINS

Turnip greens are the leafy tops of the turnip root. The leaves are somewhat bitter, as are rape and mustard greens. Bitter or not, they make good eating, especially when paired with milder varieties such as collard or kale for a belly-warming pot of mixed greens. All of these greens freeze well, so purchasing large quantities when on sale will benefit your wallet and your body.

Give a shout out to India for giving us rape with its peppery, pungent flavor and odor. Particularly strong flavored are large rape leaves. The odor can sting the inside of the nose when it begins to boil. This is a clear indication that the rape is a little long in the tooth but still edible. Like turnip greens, mix rape with collards or kale unless bitter greens are your thing.

All of these greens require real cooking, not just steaming. My first encounter with collards was disastrous. They were muddy with long inedible stems. Unfortunately, I cooked the stems and leaves—a real no, no. Well, that was thirty-five years ago. Today's greens are basically clean, that is not to say that they don't have to be rinsed a time or two.

CONVERSING IN TERMS OF GREEN

Collards, the ungratefuls refused to murmur a pleasant word to me. They squirmed and yelled obscenities when I was preparing them for cooking. Foolish person that I was, I totally ignored them. Well, they fixed my hash by being as tough as leather. The next time I prepared collards I engaged them in cordial conversation that began in the store.

"Um, you sure look nice and tender. Your leaves are such a beautiful green," I said to a bunch of collards.

"We will give you a memorable performance if you will follow our directions," one small delicate leaf said shyly.

The rest of the greens in the display cube chorused, "Yep, yep. We will be lip smackin' good." When a pot of fresh greens turns out well, you are cooking for real.

"I promise." I said soothingly.

As I was leaving the greens display cube with five pounds of each of my friends collards, kale, mustard, and turnip greens I heard the remaining greens say to me, "Y'all come on back now, ya hear?"

At home they chorused, "Here's the deal…" I was told what to do and, a compliant me, did as instructed. You too will benefit greatly by adhering to their instructions.

Greens are really happy when cooked with ham bones. Bones often make additional seasoning unnecessary. So get some good seasoning meat—preferably country ham bones and plop them into a pot of boiling water. Cook until the water becomes brownish or grayish. Again, for health conscious folks, use whatever seasoning meat works for you.

Fill a sink half full of cold water. Get out your cutting board and a sharp knife with a medium length blade. Run the knife along both sides of the stem through to the middle of the leaf. Pull out the stem and discard. The leaves will lie quietly on the board. Roll several leaves into a tight package. Cut three lines vertically (lengthwise) down each roll. Next, cut the leaves horizontally (across) into thin strips. Place the cut leaves in the cold water. Dip and rub, rub and dip several times. This will remove any foreign bodies. Just kidding.

Seasoning meat often replaces other meat for the meal, especially smoked turkey wings and necks.

BUYING GUIDE: It is sometimes difficult to determine whether greens will be tough. An excellent guide to purchasing tender greens is to select only small to medium sized leaves. Remove any long stems in the store. Most stores have receptacles for this purpose. (Why pay for something you can't eat?) Scrutinize the bunched greens. They often have rotting leaves in the center of the bunch. Avoid wilted greens. Ask the clerk if fresher ones are available and if not, look for something else. Yellowing greens are totally unacceptable; purchase frozen ones instead.

STORAGE: Refrigerate greens immediately and for no longer than a day. Cooking or blanching greens before freezing will prolong their enjoyability. Otherwise, buy only what you can consume in a day or two.

CABBAGE

Having been with us for eons, cabbage, by the first century CE, had grown into what we have today. Cabbage doesn't have a preference as to how it is served. It just wants to be on the table.

VARIETY IS THE SPICE OF LIFE

The most popular varieties of cabbage are green and white, those stripped of their green leaves, red, Chinese (bok choy), and Savoy. This wonderful vegetable can be eaten raw, boiled, fried, rolled, and stuffed. It tends to have a strong odor, so get out the air freshener. Cut up cabbage makes a hearty vegetable soup. If you prefer, there is cabbage juice. Yes, I know, that is going out on a limb. The ever-popular bold and hearty green and white cabbage can grow to the size of a large pumpkin. Just to test its goodness, I purchased such a head of white cabbage and was not disappointed. What I didn't count on was ending up with enough cabbage to feed the whole neighborhood.

Savoy cabbage is crinkly with a delicate flavor. It cooks down to nothing in a few minutes, so don't count on one head serving four people. Red is next in line flavor wise. Its mildness makes it a great addition to salads. My first encounter with red cabbage was when I lived in Germany. There, I learned to cook it gently (little water and a slow boil) which helps retain the flavor and color.

A few decades ago, some ingenious person presented us with ornamental cabbage. It is fine for decorating the yard, but this variety is not edible. Not to worry, this cabbage is only sold in nurseries and landscaping stores.

ANOTHER HELPING OF CABBAGE, PLEASE!

Cabbage is the everyday person's vegetable. It's cheap and it goes a long way. It is loaded with vitamins and is oh-so-tasty. I prefer white heads, but cabbage with green leaves works well too. Just remember to cut the green leaves in smaller strips and add to cooking water first. After about ten minutes, sachet on over to the stove and let the white leaves cozy up to the green ones. Cabbage does not freeze well so don't buy it in bulk.

A few spin-offs of cabbage are kohlrabi, cauliflower, broccoli, and the teeny, tiny Brussels sprouts.

BUYING GUIDE: All cabbage should be firm with leaves tightly pressed into one another. Savoy is a little less firm than the other varieties. Avoid any cabbage that looks wilted or has brown or yellow spots on the leaves. However, if that size head is what you prefer, pull those leaves off and put them in the store waste bin. Check the stalk end for signs of age. If it is soft, move on to another head.

STORAGE: Cabbage wrapped in plastic can be stored in the fridge for a few weeks. Cabbage can then be plopped in the vegetable bin or stored on a shelf in the fridge.

BOK CHOY

Listen up people! In this vegetable you have over six thousand years of cultivation. This vegetable traveled around Asia for quite some time—first in China where it was used for medicinal purposes, then on to Korea for Kimchi, and finally to Japan for use in stir frying. These days, bok choy can be found in local markets worldwide.

Chinese cabbage, also known as *Bok Choy*, is anything but round. Thick green leaves top off a wide white bunch of stalks attached at the base. The flavor is light and sweet with good nutritional value. Bok Choy adds flavor and crispness to Chinese stir fry dishes.

TEACH ME TODAY

I was feeling a bit puffy the day I was introduced to bok choy. I knew that to shed a few pounds I would need to slide into a reduced good-stuff diet. I always considered dieting an unpleasant experience until I heard a whimper from the bok choy that lay gracefully in the display bin.

"You look a little beat today."

"Yes, I know, I've been contemplating a diet so that I can look sleek and slinky in my new red dress."

"Fear not my lady! I will tell you how to eat until you are full and not gain an ounce."

"Please tell me more," I said in a hushed voice. This was going to be my secret at least until I tested it.

"Here's what you do."

"Uh, huh, uh, huh," I said as the bok choy rattled off the other ingredients I would need to purchase.

I was eager to prepare my meal with my lifesaving friend at the helm.

"It's time to begin slicing and dicing," the bok choy leaves said humorously.

So, I did just that and lo and behold, the finished dish was a hit with me and my slim and trim husband. We ate to our hearts content and I never worried about adding to my not so flattering waistline.

My bok choy friends taught me how to make several stir fry dishes that included only small amounts of meat. Hey, that was good for the budget too. After a week of these and other nourishing foods, I lost five pounds. Look out dress here I come.

BUYING GUIDE: Purchase only as much as you will use for the dish. Check the leaves carefully for freshness.

STORAGE: Bok Choy cannot be stored for more than a few days.

CAULIFLOWER

HERE COME THE ROMANS

Here we go people! I'm going to try to slide you into loving cauliflower. The Romans claimed that the lowly, at that time, cauliflower originated in Cyprus. Who would be a better authority than the Romans on where anything began? I tell you if it weren't for the Romans always on the move much of what we eat would still be a mystery to most of the western world.

SNIPPET TIME

Louis the XIV elevated cauliflower to a decadent dish served with veal and ham in a rich cream sauce or with sweetbreads, mushrooms, and foie gras.

Mark Twain had a cutesy phrase: "Cauliflower is nothing more than a cabbage with a college education." Well, Mr. Twain, I must agree with you. Recently, cauliflower has again been elevated by ingenious chefs who understand the importance of variety on the veggie chain.

Since the 1940's, Americans have neglected cauliflower because most people don't like the look or taste of it. Well, my friends you are in for a treat. And, I venture to guess that once you have tried my recipes you will wonder why you haven't eaten this somewhat cabbagy tasting vegetable before.

Buying Guide: Pearly white heads ensure freshness on your plate. Brown or black spots are a no, no. Talk about tight, the fresher the head the tighter the florets. Sometimes, the green leaves will curl over the cauliflower, but that is mainly at farmers' markets. Fresh is always better and less expensive because it increases the bottom line.

Storage: If not wrapped in plastic, do so at home and store anywhere in the fridge. Use within a week. Leftovers can be frozen.

KOHLRABI

It was first grown for human consumption in Germany. Rapidly spreading to other countries in 1554 to the delight of the populous in England, Italy, Spain, and finally in Tripoli, Libya.

I'M A FAST GROWER

A very productive plant, Americans learned to enjoy kohlrabi around the early nineteenth century, but because it grew so fast and furious, it didn't catch on well. This relatively new veggie in the current American marketplace is light green in color and has a somewhat sweet taste reminiscent of young cabbage or turnips hence the term "cabbage turnip" as described by the Germans. The bulb has at least two stalks growing from its sides ending with dark green foliage. Yes, it is an unusual looking specimen but I will try anything once. Never disdain a food just because it looks strange, or maybe *different* is a better description.

TAKE ME IN YOUR HANDS

My adventurous nature led me to the kohlrabi display in one of my local grocery stores. There they lay with their hairy bulbs and long stems, but I was not deterred. Having traveled so far from its origins, the kohlrabi has adopted a dialect all its own. I scarcely know how to describe what sounded like gibberish, but when it rolled into my outstretched hands, I knew I must try it.

I have since learned that kohlrabi sometimes presents without the leafy stems, which is alright too. Young leaves can make a nice pot of greens with the bulbs thrown in.

Roasting kohlrabi bulbs with carrots and potatoes around a nice piece of beef is my favorite way to serve it. The meat juices bring out the savory flavor of these vegetables.

BUYING GUIDE: Small kohlrabi bulbs retain their somewhat sweet flavor better than larger ones do. Short or no leaves, no matter. Kohlrabi is not so different in flavor and texture than turnips, so don't go overboard when purchasing them.

STORAGE: Empty from plastic store bag and toss in the vegetable bin for no more than a few days.

BRUSSELS SPROUTS

Brussels, Belgium, is home to the delectable green balls known as Brussels sprouts. England, France, and the good old U. S. of A didn't jump into the growing fray until the 1800's. Like asparagus, Brussels sprouts are not popular with the everyday man and woman on the street. I'm going to try to change that.

HOW DO MY BAUBLES GROW?

They are most often referred to as "little cabbages" but this is somewhat of a misnomer. Brussels sprouts grow on a wide round beanstalk type thingy. Little baubles, I call them, sprout all over the stalk, and from my experience, the Amish grow the largest, sweetest ones I have ever had the pleasure of eating.

These baubles are loaded with nutritional goodies. Many people don't like them because the frozen ones, and those out of season, can be bitter. Since I am a fanatic about fresh vegetables, I have found that fresh Brussels sprouts are at their finest from spring through mid-summer. Cook and eat them immediately after purchasing for superior flavor.

I SING, YOU SING

Happy Brussels sprouts get even happier when you sing to them. Before I could decide what to sing, I heard, "Hit it gorgeous!" from the baubles rolling around in my large colander.

"Give me a minute, I'm working on it," I replied.

"Tell you what, how about some elevator music? You know, easy listening stuff," they said.

"I can do that. Let's see, umhumph," I cleared my throat, opened my mouth, and to my surprise out came a nice melody. Pleased with my selection, the baubles unabashedly rolled into the pot of hot water.

BUYING GUIDE: If an Amish market is not available in your area, then purchase only loose Brussels sprouts at your local grocery store. No yellow leaves and no brown spots, please. Leaves should be tight, not loose like a fan. Recently, markets have begun carrying the sprouts still attached to the stalk for your picking pleasure.

STORAGE: Shake them out of the store's plastic bag into a heavier plastic bag. Squeeze out air. In the vegetable bin, they will last for at least a week. I *do not* recommend freezing Brussels sprouts.

ASPARAGUS

Ah, the good life. Asparagus is a very delicate edible member of the lily family. This is a vegetable from the Gods, or so the ancient Greeks proclaimed. Then the Romans got in on the act. Those loquacious orators were jumping up and down when they experienced the unique flavor, texture and, here we go again, medicinal qualities of asparagus. Well they may have been on to something. For umpteen years, dried asparagus has been used as a diuretic by Native Americans.

HELLOOO, EPICURUS

The Romans, using their fast chariots, took asparagus to the Alps. Soon they established another reason for making whoopee. They set aside a day to revere Epicurus. Epicurus, though Greek, was the first person to eschew fast food for the delicacies of life, which is why the Romans, big on feasts, decided to honor him. Oh boy, pickle a weed and become a god.

Understandably, the legions were tired of eating on the run while conquering and pillaging, so a good meal was a luxury, especially when it included asparagus prepared using Epicurus' recipe. Sadly, his recipe has been lost for the better part of ten centuries. Serving asparagus has been known to hasten ones rung on the social ladder.

Asparagus has become an international food. It is grown in England, Russia, Poland, Syria, Spain, and good old Stidham, Oklahoma. Those clever Chinese creatively candy this elegant vegetable.

EBULLIENT AND ELEGANT

To prepare asparagus, I was told by an ebullient stem, "Please don't overcook us. You will ruin our flavor and texture. Pretty us up a bit and allow our rich flavor to caress your taste buds."

"How?" I asked with anticipation.

"Get Frenchie with it. When we are young and tender peel a portion of our stem before cooking. After all, we are not a vegetable that is served with burgers. We compliment exquisite meals."

I learned early on that obedience works wonders with food. Veggies are a particularly demanding group of foods.

"Simply plop us in boiling water for a few minutes, remove us from the heat, let us stand for several minutes, and then drain and slather us with butter. If you are adventurous, rinse, pat dry, and serve us raw in salads. Or, marinating is an option."

I was young and foolish so I asked, "Marinated?"

"Oh, dear," one of the tips giggled. "It's sort of like wash, trim, pat, and pour. Are you with that?"

"Pour what?" Immediately I realized that was a stupid question.

"Duh! Dressing."

"Okay." I said, and eagerly added marinated asparagus bundles to my spectacular meals.

BUYING GUIDE: Some grocers haven't learned to place the cut end of asparagus in water. *Hey*, produce managers, asparagus retains its freshness longer in water because it has flower properties.

Tiny to medium asparagus are best served as a side dish for a special dinner. The tiny stalks, ahhh, they are the prize accompaniment to filet mignon. Large tips go well in salads. Carefully select the firmest stems and tips. Woody* stems and soft tips are inedible. Leave them for the store garbage collector.

STORAGE: Avoid storing asparagus for more than a day or two in the vegetable bin or on a shelf in the refrigerator. Wrap a damp paper towel around the base of the stems, place in a plastic bag and squeeze out the air before closing the bag. The sooner they are on your plate the better.

GREEN BEANS AND ASSOCIATES

String Beans, Haricots Verts – French for very young green beans and Yellow Wax Beans

Can you believe that green beans were once a seasonal vegetable? Now that we have gotten away from using them as ornamental plants, they are served worldwide every day. It wasn't the Romans who spread this veggie, it was the Spaniards, or so the story goes.

Green beans are loaded with vitamin A, and a pretty good amount of calcium. Back in the day, green beans really did have strings running the length of their pods. Cross pollinating has given us the hearty, nearly stringless bean we have today. Nothing wrong with that—it saves prep time and embarrassment when served.

FRENCH ME BABY!

I promised myself and ten other people that as long as I lived I would never *French style* another green bean. When I was a child, every family reunion was held at our house. My mother would cook her incredible *French style* green beans.

French style means cutting the beans lengthwise in back of the string seam. Sullenly, I French cut a bushel of fresh green beans for each reunion.

As much as I pleaded with her, my mother was adamant about not changing to another veggie. One day I was blessed with a bad cold. Blessed you say? I really was because my mother had to French those little buggers. We never had French style green beans again. Oh, happy days!

MY NEGLECTED FRIENDS

A particularly gray, cold day put me in a somber mood as I trekked to the super market. You guessed it, I'm a *sun* person. Naturally assuming that one or more vegetables would cheer me up, I walked from one display cube to another, sad-eyed and waiting for the perfect vegetable to converse with. I expected the green beans to lighten my mood, but they too gave me the silent treatment. To have fun with me they surreptitiously rolled over each other. Now I knew I wasn't entirely over the edge, so I watched closely. Suddenly, they broke out in gales of laughter.

"Tested your sanity, didn't we?"

"Not amused, I shot back. I am not interested in purchasing any green beans today. Now, laugh at that."

"Sooorry, we made a big mistake. We have been so neglected lately. Everyone is opting for our canned version. Please gather us into your bag."

They were referring to the plastic bag I had been carrying around.

The little devil on my shoulder whispered that it was my turn to have a bit of fun.

"I think I'll use your canned cousins. You know that you become cousins when they dump your butts in a can." I rattled on and on.

Finally, they begged, "We promise not to misbehave ever again."

I smiled gamely and bagged up several pounds of my green friends. I made it a family affair by throwing in a few yellow wax beans for a colorful dish. Use the same cooking method for both green beans and wax (yellow) beans.

BUYING GUIDE: Limp beans are, simply put, *old* beans. Snap one bean to test for crispness. Do not pick up handfuls of beans unless they look extraordinarily fresh; pick them one at a time. Crispness, good color, and unblemished skin are the keys to purchasing the best beans.

STORAGE: Store the beans up to four days in a good plastic bag in the fridge. They don't necessarily have to be stored in the vegetable bin. By all means buy in bulk for blanching and freezing for future use.

FRESH GREEN LIMA BEANS

It is thought that green lima beans are indigenous to Guatemala. Here again is a vegetable that was not always used for human consumption. But, who cares. These creamy delights nestled in their pods are astoundingly appetizing when incorporated with other veggies or served alone.

Today, only in the summer at farmers' markets can you purchase the freshest taste-tempting green lima beans. Check those sold in super markets carefully for wrinkled skin and black spots. Commercially, they are described as baby or large lima beans. I prefer baby limas. Frozen green lima beans are almost as good as fresh. The key word here is *almost.* Your taste buds may not even notice the difference.

These same beans when dried turn a light tan and are called *butter beans.* They make a hearty soup. A variation of green lima beans are the southern speckled butter beans, a grayish bean with light brown spots usually cooked with okra. These beans are also served as a side dish.

OH, WHAT A DREAM

    I love lima beans and you will too if you listen to them. They are so easy going. Lima beans are like an old-time choir, *soft and smooth*. They don't yell or get excited. Not surprisingly, they are much maligned because like dried beans, they sometimes create a bit of intestinal discomfort. The trick to avoiding the discomfort is to cook lima beans slowly and thoroughly or take an antacid before you eat them.

    On with the show! A breezy day in July helped me clear the cobwebs from my mind so that I could finally concentrate on a menu for the annual family gathering. Hallelujah! I finally made the decision to have a country menu featuring fresh green lima beans. Their creamy mint green would add another colorful, fiber-rich dish to complement the rest of the menu.

    I raced to the farmer's market to purchase a large quantity of fresh green lima beans and some other veggies on my list. Frantically searching stall after stall without success, I felt dejected and was ready to leave empty handed. Then from out of nowhere, some lima beans in the only basket left, not wanting to attract the attention of other buyers, quietly said, "Pssst, looking for us?"

    How did they know? Did I have pictures of them in my eyes? Whatever the means of locating me, I was happy. I literally flew around the table to the beans of my dreams. Just as

I approached the table, a little old lady sounding like the wicked witch snatched up the basket of my lovelies.

"Tom look at these lovely limas," she screeched.

To which he replied, "Woman put that basket down, I'm too tired to carry anything else. Let's go."

The old woman reluctantly placed the basket back on the table and shuffled away. At that moment my heart soared and my hope of having fresh green lima beans for my family became a reality.

"How, did you know I was looking for you?"

"We peeped at your list as you raced by us earlier."

I paid the farmer and gathered the basket of lima beans in my arms, hugging the basket like it contained gold. I was a happy camper. I sang all the way home.

Dumping them into a newly purchased large wire strainer for rinsing, I pleaded,

"Friends, please don't embarrass me. I want this to be a special country meal for my family."

The green lima beans were very supportive as they asked, "What would you like us to do?"

"Is it asking too much of you to play fair and come out creamy and quiet?"

They conferred for a minute. "We want to assuage your fears. All we ask is that you promise to be gentle with us. No hard boiling. We give our best performance when we're simmered, buttered, and allowed to thicken on our own."

"I can do that. I want to please you my friends."

"Then it's a deal. We would shake on it if we had hands. So a nod of your head will seal the deal," they said softly.

I nodded my head and prepared the best fresh green lima beans of my life. Now you can too.

BUYING GUIDE: Look for bright green beans with silky, taut skin. Brown spots or shriveling skin indicates old beans or beans that have been exposed to the heat of the sun too long. Be careful of too much bruising. Purchase small to medium lima beans. The larger ones can be starchy but they are excellent in soups.

STORAGE: Keep lima beans dry at all times. Place them in a plastic bag and store them in the vegetable bin or near the bottom of the refrigerator for no more than a few days.

EGGPLANT

I call eggplant the "purple passion" vegetable, but it also grows in white and yellow varieties. Some countries grow white and black eggplants, but not so much here. In America we grow only its famous purple brethren.

Eggplant is a member of the poisonous nightshade family, specifically, the belladonna plant. Some varieties of eggplant are High Bluish Select—bell types; Mirabel and Mini fingers—cylindrical; Sicilian—round and purple; and the striped Japanese—cylindrical. Colors range from white to jet black. Purple is the most popular color internationally.

IN HOW MANY LANGUAGES CAN EGGPLANT BE SAID?

Eggplant works well in numerous international dishes that are favorites of mine, such as Italian—Eggplant Parmesan, French—Ratatouille and that delightful Greek dish Moussaka. As a child, and with my own children, French fried eggplant was a staple.

If you have only eaten them in the traditional way, batter-fried eggplant will appease your appetite with a marvelous taste and texture. This delicious side dish can be fried, grilled, baked, and curried.

BUYING GUIDE: Purchase only plump, heavy, unwrinkled eggplants that are firm to the touch. *Do not* buy spongy eggplant. Check the green hat on the top of the eggplant. If it is dried out, the eggplant is playing dodge ball with freshness. Avoid eggplants that are too large, because that means the usually soft seeds have hardened and the meat will likely be bitter.

STORAGE: Eggplant will survive anywhere in the refrigerator. For best results cook within three or four days.

SQUASH

The Vegetable, Not the Game

At last a vegetable that is native to America. Go America! Most varieties of squash have been eaten since way back, but in some parts of America, other varieties have only recently been eaten. Popular types of nutty-flavored winter squash are acorn, butternut, and turban with its hazelnut flavor.

Technically, squash is a fruit and a vegetable, *why...?* because botanists have type cast squash as "pepo" a special type of berry that has both male and female properties. Those of us who enjoy the sweet flesh of squash consider it a vegetable because it has edible seeds according to someone who knows as much about this as I do—which is not much. Still confused? So am I but who cares we foodies will continue to speak of squash as a vegetable.

Long, long ago squash flowers were historically pollinated by North American squash bees, but pesticides wrecked that system. Soon after their demise, some ingenious commercial growers began pollinating squash using European honey bees. The law in America allows squash growers to keep one honey bee hive on their property for pollinating squash flowers and where they are scarce, hand pollination is done. Ugh, messy and tedious.

Recently, I planted yellow squash seeds, to use their flowers for my tea party, and was rewarded with an abundance of flowers and beautiful squash—no pollinating done by hand or bees. I just planted them and told them to do their thing. They made the husband happy too, he loves fried yellow squash.

The most popular summer squash is the yellow crookneck whose neck is mostly straight now from straining to see what's going on in other parts of the garden. Squash ranges in shapes from scalloped pattycake to the elongated yellow squash, and colors from green to brown.

YELLOW CROOKNECK SQUASH

Originally, yellow crookneck squash was a summer vegetable. The terms winter and summer are deceptive because those terms no longer apply since imported veggies provide us with all varieties of squash year round. The difference is that summer squash has thin soft skin and flesh while winter squash is hard inside and out.

Crookneck is a delectable variety of summer squash. It resembles a gourd with a long, slender, curved neck and a large bottom. The skin is smooth when young and becomes slightly bumpy as the squash matures from light to deep yellow. The flesh has a mild, delicate flavor. This veggie lovingly envelopes your tongue and melts in your mouth. It can be pared with zucchini for a colorful healthy side dish. My experience with this, and all squash, summer and winter, has always given me a pleasurable sense of change to an ordinary meal.

You too, as I once was, are probably under the misconception that zucchini is a squash. Not so. Zucchini is a member of the cucumber family. Old Chris Columbus, Isabella and Ferdinand's friend, started the zucchini craze in Europe when he took some of the seeds back to the Mediterranean. There zucchini is used in a myriad of dishes.

Crookneck/yellow squash flowers make an exciting side dish. These flowers can only be bought at farmer's fields. Unless you have made friends with a farmer who grows squash and can implore him to bring some to his market stall. If you are into planting, follow seed packet instructions and grow your own to have as many flowers as you have room to grow squash bushes. Their flavor is unusual; they taste like oysters to me. For anyone who is allergic to oysters as I am, this is an excellent substitute.

MOTHER KNOWS BEST

"Mama, do you think we will grow into beautiful squash like you?" asked the incredibly lovely squash flowers.

"Yes, my darlings. You will be even more beautiful than I am."

The mother yellow crookneck squash swayed on her fuzzy green stem while assuring all of her little ones that soon they would be beautiful squash. Mothers are like that.

Several weeks later, the farmer walked through his squash patch and selected only those on the fringe of maturity including those who had questioned their over-the-hill mother.

The mother wept silently, speaking courageously to her babies, "See I told you, you are among the most beautiful of all the squash in the patch."

"But we don't want to leave you, Mama."

"My darlings go out there and make me proud."

The farmer crated his squash and drove off to market. At the open-air farmer's market he proudly displayed his prized squash.

I sauntered through the aisles of veggies, not really looking for anything in particular, but listening for a veggie that I could engage in a conversation.

"Lady, look at us, we are petite and sweet."

When I heard this, I thought I might as well take a peek.

"Over here!"

They knew they had my attention. Near the middle of a table full of veggies stood a container of yellow crookneck squash winking at me with that one eye on their bottoms. I smiled and reached for the container. Pretending to sniff the cuddly little squashes, I listened intently as they told me the story of their mother's encouragement.

Old soft hearted me, I said, "Alright cuddlies, let's go home. If you don't mind I'll mix some zucchini with you."

BUYING GUIDE: Squash that has stayed too long at the dance will have bumps on it. The skin of the best squash is smooth, light yellow, and blemish free. The darker the color, the older the squash. Slight bruising is okay. Again, small to medium size squash will melt in your mouth. Larger squash have not-so-tender seeds. Not hard but not tender either.

STORAGE: Release the squash from the store's plastic bag and store loosely in the vegetable bin for no longer than three days.

SPAGHETTI SQUASH

Ah, Spaghetti squash. This oval yellow squash is a real treat. Again, it is a veggie that comes in other colors from ivory to orange. Because it is a good source of Vitamin C, it adds another much needed, nutritious veggie to meals. Enjoy a serving or two of the slightly sweet, crisp-tender texture of spaghetti squash strands.

The spaghetti squash has several names: noodle squash in England and Sharkfin in China. It used to be a winter vegetable but is now sold in grocery stores year-round.

LA,LA,LA,LA,LA

I recognized a song from a well-known opera ringing in my ears. The operatic voices repeated the melodious refrain several times. It sounded so soothing that I followed the song to...*what?* Singing spaghetti squash? Oh, my, I thought, am I really losing it? Several oval, yellow things joined the Pavarotti sounding one and sang even louder as I approached them.

"Hush," I said. "Give me the 411 on why you are singing to me?"

"Touch me," the Pavarotti sounding one ordered in heavily accented English.

Instead of touching it, I picked Pavarotti up. The skin was smooth, yet hard. As I bounced it around in my hands, I noticed that it was heavy too. Looking at the sign on the rack, I was intrigued. Spaghetti Squash $.79 per pound.

One of the other tenors spoke to me saying, "Now for seventy-nine cents a pound, you can afford to give us a try."

Gullible cook that I am I knew that I must try them. I warned them, "If you weigh more than three pounds, you stay here. Understand?"

"Pick me, pick me!" they sang out.

I thought it only proper to select Pavarotti. His strong tenor voice made me want to connect with this adorable vegetable.

At home, I rinsed the spaghetti squash, wiped it dry, and stared at it. Finally, I said in my sexiest voice, "Come on and tell me what to do, big boy."

Pavarotti chuckled and said in his steamy tenor, "Rub my booody with oil and bake me at 350°F until I'm tender. Slice me, slice me, slice me. Oops, I forgot myself, slice me in half lengthwise," he said cooing in my ear.

When I am done, remove my seeds and rake me with a fork. I was smitten. I stood there enthralled. Pavarotti broke the spell with "I tink you got it, now use your imagination to finish me off."

"Thank you my love," I said. With great care, I happily followed his instructions to the letter. No challenge here, it was smooth sailing all the way.

When I removed the spaghetti squash from the oven, I proceeded with Pavarotti's instructions. Fork in hand, I removed the seeds and raked the stringy squash meat into two bowls until I reached the skin. I was really getting into this raking thing. I started singing in a soprano voice that was not fit for human ears.

To the first bowl I added two tablespoons of butter and tossed well. Um, um good.

Now, it was time to experiment with the other bowl of these delightfully tasty strands.

BUYING GUIDE:	It is difficult to determine the age of hard-skinned vegetables. So select only small to medium spaghetti squash with smooth skin. They are not fragile, so examine them thoroughly for soft spots. *Do not* buy orangey or large ones, as they have seen better days and tend to be less sweet and not so tender.
STORAGE:	Store anywhere in the refrigerator for up to two weeks.

RUTABAGAS, PARSNIPS, AND TURNIPS

In the 1700's rutabagas, parsnips, and turnips traveled from Europe to America with immigrant farmers. Rutabaga, a Scandinavian veggie has a delicate sweet taste. Long ago, some misguided souls thought that rutabaga was only fit for animal feed. What a shame! I'm sure out of hunger they smartened up and began cooking this nourishing vegetable.

Boy, oh, boy, rutabagas are the hardest veggie in the world to peel. The slippery wax coating doesn't help at all. Rutabagas are often referred to as yellow turnips, probably because people can more readily identify with turnips. Like parsnips and turnips, rutabagas are in a not-so-popular category of vegetables. I don't know why because they are packed with nutrition and they taste so good. Ah, yes, I do know why, unlike staples such as potatoes and carrots most cooks ignore these old-fashioned, great tasting root vegetables because they don't know how to cook them.

PARSNIPITY

Parsnips are a relative of the celeriac and parsley family. They look like albino carrots with brownish tinged rings on their skin. Roasted with other root vegetables, they elicit pleasant moans from your taste buds. Buy small firm ones. Larger ones, although still firm, have a strong flavor. A bit of sugar will quiet their macho flavor. Peel and trim parsnips with a vegetable peeler as you would carrots. Peel rutabagas and turnips with a knife. All of these veggies can be roasted alone or with dense meats such as beef.

JUMPIN' JEHOSHAPHAT

As usual, select only the firmest of these vegetables. They are so neglected that when they see someone looking at them with the prospect of being purchased they go nuts.

"Don't just stand there looking at us, hurry, do the firmness routine. Maybe if others see you playing with us they'll want to get in the game."

Their excitement transcended the air between us and I was hooked. I purchased one rutabaga and three each of parsnips and turnips.

At home I decided to cook just the large rutabaga. As I was preparing to rinse it the voice still hot with excitement said, "Peel me first."

I wrestled with that rutabaga for ten minutes trying to peel it. Finally, I succeeded. From this experience I learned to buy only the smaller ones. They are easier to handle. Now it was time to cut it up. Since I wasn't strong enough to cut through it, I whacked off pieces until the job was done.

Sarcastically, I said, "Thought you could out do me, didn't ya?"

One of the pieces said, "We ain't finished with you yet."

"What do you mean?"

"What are your plans for cooking us?"

"I'm going to boil you."

"Then what?" another whacked-off piece asked.

Triumphantly I said, "Then I will season and serve you hot."

"I don't think so, we don't need any seasoning," one of the chunks said in a singsong manner.

In a contrite voice I asked, "What should I do?"

"Just boil us until very tender, drain, and mash us with a bit of butter and serve us up."

"That's all? No seasoning required?"

"Yessss," they said humoring me.

I was pleasantly surprised at the finished dish. My kids raved over it. I love those kids; they have their mother's good taste.

BUYING GUIDE:	Select small rutabagas. They are very hard and heavy. The skin is covered with a thin wax coating to prolong their freshness and protect them during travel to the store.
STORAGE:	Plop them in the refrigerator storage bin. They will last for a few weeks.

MAIZE/CORN

There is corn and then there is corn. Maize has been a staple in Native American diets since prehistoric times. The seeds of the maize plant are called kernels. Technically, a grain, maize is a nutritious starchy vegetable. Its ability to grow in diverse climates has made maize popular worldwide. The Native Americans planted maize in a complex system known as *Three Sisters*. The system begins by planting maize that provides support for beans, the beans provide bacteria that live on the bean roots that nourish the other plants and squash provides ground cover to inhibit weeds and evaporation by shading the soil. Now, that is called "killing three birds with one stone."

THE SPREADING OF MAIZE

The many varieties of maize, established since the early 1250's BCE in the Americas can be attributed to the difference in soil content. European explorers rushed back home to introduce this sugar-rich product to their homies. Its taste was not exaggerated. So wonderful was this new thing that word spread like wildfire and, before they could bat an eye, everyone in Europe was singing the praises of maize, which they renamed *corn* because they originally classified it as a cereal.

There are many varieties but only five purposes: sweet corn for human consumption; field corn for animal and plant use; ornamental corn for decorations to welcome fall; a special hard popcorn for us while watching a good movie; and for bio fuel.

From dried corn kernels known as hominy comes the ever-popular southern dish "grits," originally known as hominy grits. Grits begin life as dried sweet corn. First stage: it is coarsely ground into grits—second stage, corn meal.

The best corn on the cob is simply prepared: cut off the top tassels and the bottom stalk. The first layer of husk leaves will fall away but do not remove the other husk leaves. Rinse and place in boiling water. This process helps the corn retain its naturally sweet flavor and nutrition more so than if cooked out of the husks. Cook until the husk leaves wilt a bit, and then watch as it is gobbled up with gusto.

LEND ME YOUR EAR

Recently, I decided to traipse through a cornfield in southern Maryland. This was a glorious experience for me. As I stood at the edge of the field, my vivid imagination took hold and I could see myself wandering through these fields looking for my true love. Soon our eyes locked in a passionate embrace. As we moved toward each other, the spell was broken. I was startled out of my reverie by "No hanky panky in here."

Alone in the field except for acres of corn I was surprised to see a tall stalk of corn lean over to me, and shake itself vigorously.
"Take your passionate vision elsewhere. I'm trying to grow here."
"How did you know what I was thinking?"
"Do you think you are the first to have that experience in our fields?"
Ashamed, I asked, "Are you saying that people do this often?"
"Every season. Romantically, he said, "the stirring breeze causes the scent of our sweetness to encircle their mind while our soft silk brushes their skin and…oh, heck, come back next week when we are ready for harvest."

STORAGE: May be refrigerated over-night—no longer. Corn loses its nutritional qualities very quickly. Corn not used by next day of purchase can be blanched and frozen.

EXOTIC MUSHROOMS

There was a time when this difficult-to-grow crop was selfishly reserved for Egyptian Pharaohs. Eventually, the French one-upped them by cultivating mushrooms in limestone quarries. Their mushrooms were the best in the world at that time. The French called them *"Champignons de Paris."* Today, farmers almost anywhere grow all varieties of the ever-popular mushrooms in production facilities. That's progress for you. Commonly available in the United States, our modern cultivation began in Kennett Square, Pennsylvania in 1896. We were a little slow in the mushroom growing department. But, catch up we did, and now with precise growing conditions we can enjoy mushrooms any time our little heart desires.

Mushrooms with their soft texture will send your taste buds into orbit when you prepare them properly. Don't be fooled by their softness, some of them have very strong flavors. The varieties are endless. Here's how to identify a few species: Oyster mushrooms have long stems; Chanterelles have a golden-orange color and resemble trumpets, and when a reddish color appears, they are then called "lobster" mushrooms; Shiitakes look like cute little hats; buttons have round white caps; portobellos large brownish caps. Portobellos are the larger version of crimini mushrooms.

All of these mushrooms have varying degrees of a sweet woodsy flavor when sautéed in butter. Most mushrooms can also be purchased in their dried form.

Shiitake, *shii* is Japanese for tree-grown mushrooms and are indigenous to China, Japan, and most of Asia. However, since the 1970's they have been successfully cultivated stateside. These "little pearls" will last forever when dried. To reconstitute them simply leave them in water until they plump up. A lottery win is needed to purchase the special "donko" shiitakes that sell for $80 to $100 per pound in Asia.

Little Known Fact: Mushrooms are the only veggie that naturally contain the sunshine vitamin D and are quite effective in cancer treatments, so I'm told.

THE GOOD LIFE

I gazed at the labels below the bin of loose mushrooms. One persnickety Shiitake said, "Are you going to buy us or stare us to death?"

I responded humbly, "I want to purchase you and several of your cousins. Will you help me choose?"

Another Shiitake snickered, "Of course we will help you. Come closer."

As I lowered my ear over the mushrooms I heard them quip, "Another newbie."

"Yes, I am a newbie." I said, indignantly.

"Don't get your panties in a bunch; we will give you all the pointers you need to enjoy our exquisite, luscious, melt-in-the-mouth goodness.

"Try mixing oyster, shiitake, and chanterelles to make an extraordinary side dish," I was told by a beautiful oyster mushroom.

The button mushrooms squealed, "We are easy to prepare too."

I said politely, "You probably are, but I'm into your exotic neighbors today."

BUYING GUIDE: Buying mushrooms is a tricky thing. The only way I have been able to determine which ones are the best is to select those that are not shriveled. Squeezing and poking doesn't apply to mushrooms. Be gentle with them.

STORAGE: Mushrooms store well in paper bags or ventilated plastic bags. Retaining their flavor is all-important, so do not keep them more than two days before cooking. They have already been without nourishment for who knows how long.

PORTOBELLO MUSHROOMS
The *Big Hat* Guys

I recently learned that Portobello mushrooms are just overgrown criminis. Well, how do you like that? Grow bigger and get renamed so that we unsuspecting lovers of these fungi think it is a totally different species. I like this marketing ploy.

Portobello mushrooms are versatile. Their meatiness allows them to be grilled, baked, broiled, sautéed, and used in place of meat. They are rich in potassium, essential amino acids, and vitamin B. The combination of being low in calories and fat-free makes them an excellent resource for those watching cholesterol and an expanding waistline. Vegans will be in veggie heaven.

Ideally, use portobellos within a few days. Avoid broken, bruised, and those with curling edges. Keep them in the original packaging and refrigerate. Contrary to the suggested method of care, I prefer gently rubbing my fingers over them while holding them under cold running water. Don't drown them in water; just let the water run over them.

I'M UNIQUE, I CAN REPLACE MEAT

I was giving the mushroom selections the once over when I saw a quivering among the big guys—the Portobellos. Because I felt they had deliberately sought my attention, I bit.

"What's with the quivering?"

The managing partner of the group spoke first in an authoritative tone, "It seems that you and other not-so-smarts have neglected to give us a try and we are tired of it. Since you look fairly intelligent, we want you to be the first to break the barrier."

"And what makes you think I want to be the first?"

Another partner reminded me that, "Last week, as our predecessors were being thrown in the garbage, they told us that you gently rubbed your fingers across them even though you didn't buy any. So here's your big chance to make us popular."

"I don't know how to prepare such huge, earthy looking mushrooms."

A low-level partner advised me to be creative. That appealed to me.

It said, "Some TV chefs use us in place of meat for burger sandwiches. And, that's okay. But, grilling is the safe way to use us. Bring us home with you and we will make your reputation flourish."

"You win," I sighed.

At home I pulled the Portobello mushrooms out of their packaging, rinsed them well, and pulled off the short stems.

I know, I know, you have been told to gently brush them. Running water over them caused them to wiggle—they were enjoying the cool bath. I laid them on my cutting board and uttered, "I'm ready! Give me this recipe that will make me a Cast Iron Chef."

"Okay, here goes!" they replied in unison.

BUYING GUIDE: Look out for curled edges, as this is indicative of mushrooms that are past their freshness date, no matter what the label says. The tops of the mushrooms should be a grayish brown color, and the underside should be black.

STORAGE: Leave them in the store container in the vegetable bin. For the best flavor and texture, do not store for more than a few days.

SUGAR BEETS, ANYONE?

    First grown in the Mediterranean, only the sugar beet leaves were eaten for many centuries. Not until the French recognized their potential in the 1800's did humans slide their tender succulent bodies into their diets. The most popular sugar beet is deep red and can be found in most local grocery stores. But, beets also come in yellow, white, and the amazing candy-stripe. Only specialty markets carry these unusual varieties.

    Beets are an excellent source of potassium and fiber. Their leaves in particular have even more nutrition. The leaves contain protein, calcium, fiber, beta-carotene, vitamins A, C, and some B. Beet leaves and bulbs are known to purify the blood and the liver, or so natural healers proclaim. Beets are a magnet for the health conscious.

    You haven't lived until you have eaten candy-striped beets. *Just messing with you*. Do you know that a great many of our prepared foods such as gravy and soup contain a powdered form of beets, and that it is an ingredient in food dye?

    Beets are the quietest vegetable. Their passiveness often translates into "leave me alone." Despite this attitude, they are versatile. They can be boiled, roasted, steamed, or eaten raw—not my favorite. They make an excellent snack right out of the jar.

If you are concerned about the beets staining your cookware, the trick is to soak the pot in vinegar for a few minutes. Stain all gone. There isn't much you can do to ruin these bashful little wonders. Roast and peel a bunch, let them cool, and enjoy their natural sweetness.

Beets are another reticent veggie. I have tried on several occasions to communicate with them but alas, no luck.

BUYING GUIDE: Firmness is key to root vegetables and beets are no exception. Stems may cause them to weigh a little more but they almost always guarantee sweetness and freshness. Unless you plan to eat them, snap 'em off and leave for the grocery store garbage.

STORAGE: Store as you would potatoes in a cool dry place in a veggie bin or at the bottom of the fridge. Cook within a week.

Starch Stories

PASTA, NOODLES, POTATOES, RICE AND GRITS

The Etruscans diddled around with pasta as far back as 400 BCE. The Italians, after having been introduced to noodles became bored, as I would too, and came up with a product of their own. Basically, they used the same ingredients but with a few twists. Over the years those geniuses found that semolina flour works best when creating a myriad of cute shaped pastas such as wheels, corkscrews, bow ties, spaghetti, shells, and macaroni to name a few.

Pasta and noodles provide just the right touch to any meal. They can be as exciting as the colorful vegetable pasta or as sophisticated as strands of angel hair pasta. Personally, I like those little bow tie and corkscrew pastas, they are so playful.

I know most of us believe that noodles originated with the Italians. Not so. There is some skepticism about Marco Polo, ingenious little scamp that he was, discovering noodles. He did bring noodles to Italy from his travels in China but that was the extent of his discovery. Was he really the first person to introduce noodles to Italy? No, while he was busy making nice with the Chinese, an unknown Genoan soldier beat him to the punch. Most people refuse to accept this, but alas, it's true.

Word to the wise: Make sure your name is on the product of your discovery when you introduce it. If not, you will be lost to history.

Anyway, before becoming president and while serving as Ambassador to France, Tommy Jefferson—a connoisseur of women and food—sampled a dish of macaroni and it was love at first bite. Ever the entrepreneur, Tommy bargained for a "ton" of macaroni ingredients and a few pasta-making machines. Tommy was a smart dude, he could foresee the huge marketing potential and dollar signs rang up in his eyes.

Down the road in 1848, a little known Frenchman built the first pasta factory in, where else? Brooklyn, New York. An industrious man at a loss for a place to dry his pasta, he let *Mr. Sunshine* do it for him on the roof of his building.

Noodles and pasta are totally different. Pasta comes in an assortment of shapes and sizes and generally does not contain eggs. Whereas, noodles come thin, medium, and wide and usually consist of flour, water, and eggs.

I AM A GOOD COOK

As my eyes scanned the pantry shelves, my mind was rolling like a race car on the Indie 500.

"Hey, Lady, down here."

My eyes went immediately to a box of vegetable pasta. "What do you want little one?"

"Can you come out and play?"

"Play what?" I asked cautiously.

"Play at being a good cook. Hee, hee, hee."

"You just wait one minute, I am a good cook."

"Yeah. In your dreams."

I was stunned at this unusual discourse.

"I prepare pasta according to the directions on the box," I said with pride.

"That's my point. You need to learn to live dangerously."

"What does living dangerously have to do with pasta?" I retorted angrily.

"Okay, maybe that was a bit over-the-top. But, lying around in a box being ignored most of your life can make you somewhat hostile. Get my point?"

"When I'm finished you will have learned to cook on the wild side for a super change to your usually dull pasta dishes."

Time for some levity I said, "Let's get started you little bump in my road."

"Bump in the road? Talk dirty to me, girly."

I laughed out loud at that one. From that day on my pasta dishes have become quite exciting.

BUYING GUIDE: Pasta and noodles have a very long shelf life. Keep several varieties on hand for last minute meals.

STORAGE: Store pasta and noodles in original packaging.

CENTURIES OF RICE

Rice has been around for thousands of years but only recently have there been numerous varieties available worldwide. Now we have Jasmine (Thai); short (Japanese and Korean); long and glutinous (Chinese and Japanese); Basmati (Indian); and Risotto (Italian) in addition to brown and saffron rice. Wild rice really isn't rice; it's the "pod" from wild grasses.

The origin of rice is still a mystery. But, over many centuries perhaps from around 2500 BCE, it has fed more hungry mouths than any other grain. In Thai culture, the myth is that rice was a gift from the gods. In fact rice is revered and is used in many elaborate rituals.

The Portuguese sailors brought rice to Brazil and the Spaniards began cultivation in Central and South American countries. Not until the late 1600's did rice production explode in the States first in South Carolina, then in Louisiana, and finally in California.

FOR THE LOVE OF A GOOD MEAL

In a happy and lovely mood, I sacheted down my favorite grocery store's prepared foods aisle not looking for anything in particular. I heard giggles behind me. Looking around I thought some kids might have been poking fun at me. I was dressed rather caribbeanish. Coordinated, yet colorful. Good moods make you do that. Anyway, when I looked around I discovered that I was alone in the aisle.

I soon realized that I was in the starch aisle. Having talked to vegetables, I wasn't reluctant to try my luck with a bag of lasagna noodles.

"Hi, there," I ventured. No response. Oh well, maybe the rice will talk to me especially since I may purchase several varieties today.

"Wait! We weren't ignoring you, we were afraid you might think us too forward."

"Forward? Do you even know the meaning of the word?"

"Well no. But we thought it sounded intelligent."

I laughed heartily and let my eyes wander a little further down the aisle. On the top shelf, I noticed an item new to me, Jasmine rice. Ever the eager-to-learn cook, I thought, hmm, maybe this will make a pleasant replacement for just plain rice. My mind sung, "Thought noted."

I continued my perusal of these carbs amazed to see how many different kinds of pasta, rice, and boxed potato items were available for quick, wholesome meals. Since making pasta at home doesn't appeal to me, I decided to try some of those little gems. Having gathered several varieties, I proudly wanted to rush home to my kitchen to experiment with them.

As I was pushing my cart toward the register, I heard quiet giggles that turned into loud laughter. I stopped in my tracks and looked into my cart. Those bags and boxes were doing the "Electric Slide" to the store's piped-in music. They looked adorable. Because no one was watching, I joined them. See, even grocery shopping can be fun. We line danced to the end of the aisle.

Old Miss Perkins heard the fun and peeped around the corner. She wasted no time verbalizing her disgust.

Glaring at me the old biddy said, "Hrumph, some people just don't have any respectability about themselves."

I gave her a wide smile and said, "Lighten up, Perky and join the fun."

Old Perkins snatched herself around and stormed out of the store. My cart full of goodies and I snickered quietly as I rolled them to the checkout counter.

In my pantry at home, I began sorting my goodies. My friends yelled simultaneously, "Use me for dinner today."

"Look I'm sorting you for storage. I'll decide tomorrow who will be first."

Then it hit me, what am I going to prepare for dinner tonight. Let's see, I have some fresh green beans and yellow crookneck squash already cooked. "Mmm," I said out loud, rubbing my chin, I can make pork chops stuffed with wild rice. If the husband doesn't like that, there's always KFC®.

As I entered the pantry to get the rice, all of the carbs began dancing a jig.

"Calm down," I said.

A box of noodles angled for my attention.

"Have you considered that I will make a nice cushion for those pork chops?"

"Another day, I have decided to use wild rice today."

"Well, if you want to be like that," the noodles said snarkily.

When my husband arrived home, the food fragrances drew him like a magnet to the kitchen. I shooed him off to the dining room table. With my usual flair, I presented this simple, nourishing meal to his rave reviews. But then, he is my husband and knows how lonely and uncomfortable the couch is in his man cave.

BUYING GUIDE: Rice has a life span of many months. Purchase a generous supple to avoid running out.

STORAGE: Store in original packaging or in a tightly sealed container.

WHITE POTATOES, GOLD POTATOES, RED POTATOES
All purpose, Yukon Gold, Red Bliss, Russet, and Yams/Sweet Potatoes

Okay, now that we have finished our bowl of pasta or rice and have taken a nap we shall enter the realm of potatoes. My, what a heavenly food! Potatoes can be baked, boiled, fried, and drowned in gravy, cheese sauce, sour cream, and butter. My favorite way to spend an evening is ensconced on my bed slurping a bowl of whipped potatoes while helping the cast of a *CSI TV* show solve a murder.

This Irish phenomenon traveled into our diets several hundred years ago and still remains a favorite. Peru and Chile can be complimented for cultivating potatoes way back in 500 BCE. They called them "papas." Can you believe that the Incas worshiped the potato as a deity?

Potatoes have long been a staple for many civilizations. The Spanish, Russian, English, and Irish are well-known potato cultivators. The lovelies were introduced to America in the 1600's and since then we have developed our own unique flair for cultivating and hybridizing them.

IMAGINE A WORLD WITHOUT POTATOES— FRIGHTFUL

There exists an old wives' tale that claims a potato will cure rheumatism. Well, friends, I have consumed enough potatoes in my life to ward off the most severe forms of rheumatism and yet I still suffer with this infamous condition. So much for old wives and their tales!

Marie Antoinette supposedly pinned potato flowers in her hair. She should have let those flowers grow into potatoes and offered them to her starving people. In hindsight, I'm sure she wished she had ordered, "Let them eat potatoes." Maybe she would have lived to a ripe old age. Oh, well!

No matter the color or variety of potato—red, white, purple, gold, fingerling, russet, or sweet—they all go "oooh," "ouch" when you scrub them. You see, the little buggers have very thin skins. Talk to them before scrubbing; they like getting a heads up. It prevents them from becoming resentful and deliberately burning. To avoid their cantankerous bellyaching, I reassure them that they will be handled with love.

"You all-purpose whites, I will make you cheesy and serve you with love. Goldies, you will be superb cooked with garlic and smashed. Russets, I will make you into rich, fluffy mashed potatoes. Purple and fingerlings, you will be boiled, seasoned lightly with French grey or sea salt, and splashed with butter."

The potatoes listened intensely. They liked the idea of being special. How do I know this? They stood on end and jumped up and down like a chorus line in a Broadway musical.

Gooey sweet potatoes (yams) are special. Holiday dinners are not complete without them. Oh, forgive me my lovelies. I don't know what I was thinking—you Russets are holiday fare too."

I simply can't bring myself to use prepared potatoes on a regular basis. I'm a cook that loves to try everything new on the market including packaged potatoes, but they just don't cut it for me. Here's a secret though, I do keep a box of instant mashed potatoes on the shelf for emergencies. I add them to fresh potatoes as a stretcher when I've run out of fresh ones. Also, if I'm hungry, in a hurry, and don't have time to cook a batch of potatoes for myself, I resort to instant, which I dress up with evaporated milk and lots of butter. So if you are in a pinch, maybe, but not on a regular basis. Potatoes in cold storage tubs are really good but a bit pricy for everyday family use.

BUYING GUIDE: Selecting potatoes, whether loose or bagged requires careful examination. Soft potatoes are inedible. They are either old or have been frozen. Potatoes that have been frozen raw will also have black spots inside—they too are inedible.

Potatoes with eyes—those nubby little things—are ready for replanting. Deep cuts in potatoes bring to mind a source for bacteria. Wash potatoes with a brush; they were plucked out of dirt. Freezing for more than a week causes fresh cooked potatoes to turn mealy. Yuk!

STORAGE: Potatoes usually fill a vegetable bin so it is unlikely you will store other vegetables with them. Avoid storage in plastic bags, as this causes potatoes to sweat and spoil quickly. Potatoes are loaded with water, so if the temperature in the refrigerator is too low, the potatoes will freeze. Use a brown paper bag to store potatoes that cannot be refrigerated and place them in a dark cool place.

Something to Ponder: Not all of us can think outside the box, but we can create our own box, which is so much better. Cooking doesn't have to be a dreaded chore. It can be fun, especially when you converse with the food.

You now have the tools to improve your cooking skills, hide your mistakes and to create laugh-out-loud conversations with food.

Don't let mishaps in the kitchen deter you from your mission to get the best bargains, prepare nutritious meals, and savor all compliments.

One Last Tip: Coupons, coupons, coupons! These little pieces of paper can save you a small fortune. Check your newspaper and online for cents-off coupons. You'll be surprised at how much you can save. With coupons in hand, purchase several items for future use. There is one catch. Sometimes a retailer will only accept their coupons, so read the advertisement carefully before you begin sniping.

Well, folks this concludes our journey into the life of Feisty Vegetables and Incredible Starches.

Enjoy the recipes!

VEGETABLE RECIPES

Nutritional Values are approximate

Fantastic Stewed Tomatoes

3 large hothouse tomatoes
6 plum tomatoes
¾ C sugar
1 stick butter
½ tsp salt
½ tsp black pepper

1 medium onion, chopped
2 ribs celery, chopped
1 clove garlic, finely chopped
1 green pepper, chopped (opt.)
3 C water

*Flour paste (aerate flour using a small whisk or folk before adding cold water)

Rinse tomatoes, pat dry. Peel onion, garlic and strip the celery*. Remove stem end of tomatoes. Rough chop hot house tomatoes, cube plum tomatoes. Set aside 1 cup cubed tomatoes. Throw all tomatoes into boiling water. Add onion, celery, black pepper, green pepper and garlic to boiling tomatoes. Reduce heat to medium high until all ingredients are soft. Add sugar, butter, salt, Simmer 15 minutes. Drizzle in flour paste until tomato sauce begins to thicken. Add those cute little tomato cubes. Continue to simmer for 15 minutes.   Serves 6.

Total Time: 35 mins.

Nutritional Values per serving

Calories 241, Total Fat 15g, Total Carbohydrates 28g, Cholesterol 40mg, Sodium 120mg, Protein 12g, Potassium 3,336mg, Fiber 2%, Vitamin A 25%, Vitamin C 60%, Iron 2%, Calcium 24%.

Corn and/or okra can be added to this basic recipe.

<u>Corn</u>: Add one 16 oz can of whole kernel corn with juice just before thickening the sauce. Stir constantly. Serves 6.

Okra: Rinse ½ pound of fresh okra. Remove tops and tips of bottoms. Slice into ½ inch rounds. In frying pan heat three tablespoons of oil and distribute okra evenly in hot pan. Stir constantly until sliminess disappears. Be careful not to brown the okra. Use a slotted spoon to remove okra from hot oil. Add to thickened tomatoes.   Serves 6.

Michael's Yummy Carrot Casserole

2 lb bag carrots
3 C water
1 C sugar (more or less depending upon sweetness of carrots)
2 T cinnamon

1 stick melted butter
1 T vanilla
2 eggs
1 small can evaporated milk
2 T nutmeg

Rinse and peel carrots with a vegetable peeler. Use food processor or mandolin to slice carrots thinly. Boil carrots until extra soft. Drain. In large bowl combine eggs, milk and sugar, beat well. Add carrots and remaining ingredients. Whip with electric mixer. Pour into casserole dish. Sprinkle additional sugar, cinnamon and nutmeg in that order over the top. Cover with pats of butter. Bake at 350° until center is set.
Serves 6.

Total Time: 1 hr.

Nutritional Values per serving

Calories. 253, Total Fat 15g, Total Carbohydrates 32g, Cholesterol 40mg, Sodium 120mg, Protein 12g, Potassium 280mg , Fiber 24%, Vitamin A 27%, Vitamin C 60%, Iron 4%, Calcium 24%.

Best Dang Hot or Cold Carrot Salad

1 lb bag carrots, thinly sliced	1 half green bell pepper, minced
2 C water	1 garlic clove, minced
1 can Tomato Bisque Soup	¼ C sugar
½ medium onion, minced	¼ C oil
1 celery stalk, minced	¼ C vinegar

Peel and slice carrots. A mandolin or food processor works best. Plop carrots into boiling water. Cook until carrots are tender. Drain thoroughly. Throw in the remaining ingredients while carrots are hot. Serve hot as a side dish or cold as a salad on green lettuce or romaine leaves. What the heck, use whatever leaves you prefer. Remember you are a creative wiz.
Serves 6

Total Time: 1 hr.

Nutritional Values Per Serving

Calories 122, Total Fat 10g, Total Carbohydrates 9g, Cholesterol 0g, Sodium 7mg, Protein 6g, Potassium 140mg, Fiber 12%, Vitamin 13%, Vitamin C 30%, Iron 2%, Calcium 1%.

Positively Smashing Smothered Onions

2 large yellow onions
¼ cup vegetable oil
¼ tsp seasoned salt
¼ tsp pepper
¼ C water

Peel yellow onions. Cut them into medium slices throw them into a bowl of cold water. Heat oil on high. Carefully add onions to hot oil. Sprinkle on seasoned salt and pepper. Cover for 8 -10 minutes. Lower heat and stir frequently until they begin to brown slightly. At this stage be careful not to do an *oops* and let them get too brown. Pour in water and cover. Let simmer until onions have caramelized*. Set aside until ready to serve.
Serves 4.

Total Time: 15 mins.

Nutritional Values per serving

Calories 120, Total Fat 14g, Total Carbohydrates 9g, Cholesterol 0mg, Sodium 0mg, Protein 1g, Potassium 170mg, Fiber 2g, Vitamin C 10%, Calcium 2%.

Margaret's Spicy Garlic Pepper Sauce

2 large cloves of garlic, minced
2 T olive oil
1 large can crushed tomatoes
1 small green bell pepper
   sliced into thin strips

1 tsp Thai chili paste
½ C heavy cream
½ tsp sugar

Heat olive oil in frying pan. Sauté garlic and pepper until garlic is golden. Pour in crushed tomatoes, sugar and chili paste. Simmer for ten minutes. Add heavy cream. Stir constantly until slightly thickened. Pour over pasta or anything else your heart desires. Serves 6.

Total Time: 30 mins.

Nutritional Values per serving

Calories 100, Total Fat 8g, Total Carbohydrates 3g, Cholesterol 27mg, Sodium 7mg, Fiber 1g, Potassium 2mg, Vitamin C 4%.

Must Have Roasted Garlic Paste

1 sleeve of garlic   1 tsp olive oil or vegetable oil

Cut garlic heads in half crosswise. Scoot into baking dish. Drizzle oil over both halves cover with foil. Bake at 350° until garlic is very soft. When done squeeze cloves into a bowl, smash, smash, smash with a fork or use a mortar and pestle*. Place in airtight container and refrigerate for use in any recipe that speaks of garlic. This recipe can be broken down into individual servings and frozen.

Total Time: 30 mins.

Nutritional Values per serving

Calories 15, Total Fat 2g, Total Carbohydrates. 2g, Cholesterol 0mg, Sodium 7mg, Potassium 2mg, Vitamin C 4%.

Sugar and Spice Leeks and Broccoli

2 medium leeks
1 bunch broccoli florets
3 T vegetable or olive oil

1 T light brown sugar
Pinch* cayenne pepper
Pinch salt

Cut off green tops of leeks and fling them into the garbage or save them for garnish. Split leeks lengthwise. Rinse each layer thoroughly. Slice across into thin strips. In frying pan heat oil, add leeks, cayenne pepper, brown sugar and salt. Mix well. Cook on medium heat until leeks are tender and sticky. Add small amount of water if stickiness persists before leeks are done. Let the broccoli crash the party. Add leftover meat of your choice to make a main dish.
Serves 2.

Total Time: 20 mins.

Nutritional Values per serving

Calories 4, Total Carbohydrates. 0g, Cholesterol 0mg, Sodium 1mg, Fiber 2g, Protein 1g, Vitamin A 5%, Vitamin C 17mg, Iron 1%.

Stir Fry Scallion Topper

2 bunches scallions (green onions, tops and bulbs)
¼ stick butter

¼ C slivered almonds, optional
1 small red bell pepper cut into thin strips

Remove root ends of scallions. Rinse and pat dry. Starting with green tops slice on diagonal through to the bulb. Place in bowl add red pepper strips. Heat butter in frying pan to foaming throw in scallions and peppers. Sauté for 2 minutes. Sprinkle in almonds. Stir to incorporate all ingredients. Serve as a topping on pastas or mix with steamed green beans. Serves 4.

Total Time: 10 mins.

Nutritional Values per serving
Calories 213, Total Fat 11g, Total Carbohydrates 29g, Cholesterol 15g, Sodium 62mg, Protein 6g, Fiber 7g, Potassium 33mg, Calcium 2%, Iron 2%, Vitamin A 8%, Vitamin C 30%.

Delectable Creamed Shallots and Spinach

1 lb small shallots (brownish skin) 1 box cooked frozen spinach
1 C heavy cream 1 T butter
1 chicken bouillon cube

Cook spinach set aside. Peel and remove root ends and tops of shallots. Slice shallots thickly. In small frying pan throw in butter and sauté shallots. Cook until tender, add cream and bouillon cube. Squeeze out water from spinach and add to cream mixture. Reduce heat and cover for 5 minutes stirring occasionally.
Serves 4.

Total Time: 15 mins

Nutritional Values per serving

Calories 75, Total Fat 6g, Total Carbohydrates 2g,
Cholesterol 20g, Sodium 1,100mg, Calcium 4%, Vitamin A 4%.

∽o∽

Nora's Cauliflower Smush

1 medium head cauliflower
¼ stick butter

¾ cup Parmesan cheese
cover with cooking

Cut off green outer leaves and end stalk. With a paring knife cut florets off the stalk, no stems, please and plop in a bowl of cold water. Rinse thoroughly. Cook until very tender. Drain well. Slide the cauliflower into a medium size bowl, add butter and Parmesan cheese. Mash those little grainy heads while incorporating the cheese and butter.
Serves 4.

Total Time: 30 mins.

Nutritional Values per serving

Calories 140, Total Fat 12g, Cholesterol 38mg, Sodium 382mg, Fiber 1gm, Protein 9gms, Vitamin A 4%, Calcium 27%.

Cauliflower and Friends

1 bag California Vegetables
   if you are in a hurry
      or
1 16oz bag baby carrots
1 small head cauliflower
2 bunches broccoli, florets only

1 small onion, chopped
1 lb green beans, snapped
1 small red pepper, sliced into
   strips
½ stick butter
½ cup ranch dressing

Throw a pot of water on the stove and cook veggies according to your desired taste (crispy or soft). Drain veggies are when done, butter them up. Stir carefully so as not to pulverize the veggies. Drizzle on ranch dressing and stir. Serve hot. Serves 6.

Now Get Creative and do some mixing and matching.

Total Time: 35 mins if fresh veggies are used.

Nutritional Values per serving

Calories 153, Total Fat 17gm, Cholesterol 27mg, Sodium 233 mg, Total Carbohydrates 1g, Protein 1g, Sugar 1g, Vitamin A 5%, Vitamin C 1%, Iron 1%.

Mr. Ed's World Famous Cabbage

1 large head of cabbage white and green leaves
2 C water
½ lb bacon
1 small onion, chopped

1 medium green bell pepper, chopped (optional)
Salt and black pepper to taste
Dash* of red pepper flakes (optional)

In large pot render* bacon. Simultaneously, remove the dark green leaves, if any, from the cabbage and rinse well. Pull out the old cutting board, roll up the green leaves and slice thinly. Set aside. Cut the remaining cabbage into quarters. Remove and throw out the core. Thickly shred each quarter with a large knife. Pull that fantastic smelling fried bacon from the pot and throw in the green leaves add water. Cook for 10 minutes, toss in remaining cabbage, onion, red pepper flakes and chopped green pepper. Cook cabbage until desired tenderness. The old fashioned way is to stir the cabbage with a long fork. Before adding salt taste to prevent over seasoning. Season with salt if necessary. Add red pepper flakes and black pepper to taste. Serves 6.

Total Time: 1 hr.

Nutritional Values per serving

Calories 17, Cholesterol 10mg, Sodium 15mg, Sugars 2g, Protein 2g, Fiber 2g, Calcium 23mg, Potassium 72mg.

Liz's Fried Cabbage

1 medium head of white cabbage
6 slices bacon
1 small onion, chopped
Salt and Pepper to taste

In a frying pan cook bacon until crisp. On cutting board slice open cabbage, cut into quarters. Remove core, cut cabbage crosswise into thick slices. Place in water. Remove bacon from frying pan. Add cabbage to hot bacon grease. Cover and fry on medium heat. After 10 minutes, stir from bottom, add onions and seasoning. Continue cooking until tender-crisp. Remove from heat. Top with crumbled bacon.
Serves 6.

Total Time: 30 mins.

Nutritional Values per serving

Calories 17, Cholesterol 20mg, Sodium 15mg, Sugars 2g,
Protein 2g, Fiber 2g, Calcium 23mg, Potassium 72mg.

Stick to the Ribs Mixed Greens

6 C water
3 large country ham bones

4 lbs each collards, turnip, rape and mustard greens
Seasoned salt and pepper to taste

Boil bones until water turns grayish. Remove seasoning meat from its now savory water. Using a sharp knife strip leaves of all greens. Throw greens into sink of cold water. Rinse well and pile the greens into the seasoned water. If pot becomes full, let the greens cook down add more. When all greens are in the pot drop bones on top of greens. Stir occasionally. Cook greens until dark and tender. Add pepper, taste water seasoned salt may not be necessary. Remove bones before serving.
Serves 8.

Total Time: 2 hrs.

Nutritional Values per serving

Calories 57, Cholesterol 0mg, Sodium 15mg, Protein 2g, Fiber 2g, Calcium 100mg, Potassium 138mg, Vitamin A 10%, Vitamin C 25%.

Collards and Cabbage

leftover collards
1 small head of cabbage (See cabbage for preparation)
2 C water

Sprinkle roughly cut up cabbage into a small amount of boiling water. Cook until soft. Add more water if necessary. Drain cabbage. Throw cooked collards with juice in with cabbage. Reheat.
Serves 4.

Total Time: 40 mins.

Nutritional Values per serving

Calories 37, Cholesterol 0mg, Sodium 15mg, Sugars 2g, Protein 2g, Fiber 2g, Calcium 23mg, Potassium 72mg.

Mmm Good Vegetarian Stir Fry

1 head bok choy, sliced crosswise
1 C carrots, peeled & sliced diagonally*
1 C slice green onions, ends removed
2 C mushrooms of your choice, sliced
1 clove fresh garlic
1 small block tofu cut into thin strips
3 T light Chinese soy sauce
1 T corn starch
¾ C water
¼ C oil

Rinse all vegetables. Slide the vegetables into a bowl of cold water. Slap garlic with flat side of knife, remove skin and mince. Heat oil in a wok or large frying pan. Shake water from veggies. Carefully place all veggies and Tofu in the heated oil. Cook 10 minutes. Meanwhile stir together soy sauce, corn starch and water. Drizzle sauce onto veggies stirring constantly until slightly thickened. Add small amount of water if sauce becomes too thick. Reduce heat let vegetables simmer for 5 minutes to absorb the corn starch taste. Serve immediately. Serves 4.

Total Time: 20 min.

Nutritional Values per serving

Calories 167, Cholesterol 0mg, Carbohydrates 7g, Sugar 0mg,
Total Fat 15g, Protein 18g, Sodium 18mg, Fiber 2g,
Vitamin A 23%, Vitamin C 34%, Calcium 1%, Iron 7%.

Jump'n Good Roasted Kohlrabi

2 lbs small bulb kohlrabi
1 medium onion quartered
¼ C Pearl River Bridge® Chinese fermented soy sauce*

3 medium carrots, peeled cut into chunks
1 C water

(Find in international section of grocery store or Asian market, if not available, do not use any other soy sauce, replace with ¼ cup melted butter)

Cut off stems and tail. Peel kohlrabi bulb and roll into cold water. Quarter bulbs and place in roasting pan or baking dish together with onions and carrots. Drizzle soy sauce or butter over vegetables. Bake covered at 350° until vegetables are tender and moist. These same veggies can accompany a roast for a one-dish meal.
Serves 4.

Total Time: 45 mins.

Nutritional Values per serving

Calories 48, Cholesterol. 0mg, Sodium 50mg,
Sugars 1g, Protein 3g, Fiber 2g, Potassium 168mg,
Calcium 12mg, Vitamin A 354%, Vitamin C 9%.

Sautéed Kohlrabi

2-3 small kohlrabi, peeled and rinsed   2 T butter
1 small red bell pepper, thinly sliced   Seasoned salt

Plop butter into a frying pan. Slice kohlrabi into medium strips. Shove kohlrabi and bell pepper into hot pan. Stir to tender-crisp. Add seasoned salt to taste.   Serves 4
Total Time: 20 mins.

Nutritional Values per serving

Calories 48, Cholesterol 0mg, Sodium 50mg, Sugars 1g, Protein 3g, Fiber 2g, Potassium 168mg, Calcium 12mg, Vitamin A 354%, Vitamin C 9%.

Plainly Speaking Brussels Sprouts

1 lb fresh Brussels Sprouts   1 C boiling water
                                     2 T butter

Slice a thin strip off the end portion of these baubles some leaf separation may occur, cook them as well. Rinse and let them slide into boiling water. Cook until tender. Drain. Toss in butter. Serves 2.

Total Time: 30 mins.

Nutritional Values per serving

Cal. 30, Cholesterol 0mg, Sodium 9mg, Sugars 7mg, Protein 3g, Fiber 1g, Potassium 133mg, Calcium 15mg.

Dressed Up Brussels Sprouts

1 lb Brussels sprouts
1 small yellow bell pepper, thinly sliced
2 T butter, browned
1 small onion, sliced lengthwise

1 medium Gala apple, peeled and chopped into small cubes
1 tsp grated ginger (optional)

Rinse and thinly slice Brussels sprouts lengthwise add to browned butter. Throw in apple, onion, ginger and yellow bell pepper strips. Cook for 10 minutes on high heat.   Serves 2.

Total Time: 30 mins.

Nutritional Values per serving

Calories 30, Cholesterol 0mg, Sodium 9mg, Sugars 7mg, Protein 3g, Fiber 1g, Potassium 133mg, Calcium 15mg, Vitamin C 12%, Vitamin A 5%.

Yvette's Sophisticated Asparagus

1 lb asparagus
½ bottle of Italian Dressing
1 gallon size plastic bag

1 small red bell pepper, cut
 into thin strips (optional)
1 carrot, peeled and julienned
1 bunch green onion tops

Discard woody end of the asparagus. Rinse and pat dry. Cut off the bulb part of the green onions. In plastic bag marinate all veggies in Italian dressing except onion tops. Coat gently. Refrigerate for an hour or overnight. Use tongs to dip the green tops into boiling water for a few seconds until limp. Let cool on a paper towel.

Bundle together four stalks of asparagus around two strips of red pepper and two carrot sticks lay veggies on green onion top wrap and tie in a cute knot.
Serves 4.

Total Time: 30 mins.

Nutritional Values per serving

Calories 65, Total Fat from 55gm, Cholesterol 10mg,
Sodium 125mg, Sugars 1mg, Protein 2g, Potassium 134mg,
Calcium 13mg, Vitamin C 12%, Vitamin A 5%.

Asparagus in Lemon Juice

1 lb small asparagus,
1 T butter

1 T fresh lemon juice (white wine may be substituted)
freshly ground black pepper (optional)

Rinse and remove woody ends from asparagus. In a hot frying pan add butter brown slightly. Add asparagus. Sauté 5 minutes. Add lemon juice and pepper. Mix well. Remove from heat, serve immediately.
Serves 2

Total Time: 15 mins.

Nutritional Values per serving

Calories 65, Total Fat from 55g, Cholesterol 10mg, Sodium 125mg, Sugars 1mg, Protein 2g, Potassium 134mg, Calcium 13mg, Vitamin C 12%, Vitamin A 5%.

Green Beans Kozy

3 lbs fresh green
1lb yellow wax beans
1 pound of seasoning meat*

1 small onion, rough chopped
seasoned salt
pepper to taste

*Smoked turkey wings, smoked neck bones, ham hocks or one country ham bone.

Cook seasoning meat in large pot with enough water to cover for at least 15 minutes. Meanwhile, pinch off ends of beans. Snap into several pieces or leave whole. Add beans and onion to boiling water. Stir occasionally. Cook until dark green and tender. Taste water before adding additional seasonings.

Some folks like to eat the meat from these bones. Go figure! Myself, I garbage all seasoning meat except smoked turkey wings which I rarely use. The wings may be served as the meat dish with this recipe.
Serves 6.

Total Time: 45 mins.

Nutritional Values per serving

Calories 80, Cholesterol 0mg, Sodium 1mg, Sugars 1g, Protein 2g, Potassium 182mg, Calcium 55mg, Vitamin A 8%.

Steamed Green Beans Almondine

2 lbs fresh small green beans
¼ C slivered almonds

1 T soy or oyster sauce

Rinse and snap off ends of green beans. Steam whole green beans for 15 minutes. Drain. Add almonds and soy or oyster sauce. Serves 6

Total Time: 30 mins.

Nutritional Values per serving

Calories 156, Total Fat 11gm, Cholesterol 0mg, Sodium 1mg, Sugars 1g, Protein 2g, Potassium 182mg, Calcium 55mg, Vitamin A 10%.

Tantalizing Green Lima Beans

2 lbs fresh or frozen green lima beans
1 stick butter
2 ½ C water, more if needed

seasoned salt
black pepper

Bring water to a boil in a large sauce pan. Add rinsed green lima beans. After 15 minutes, add butter, seasoned salt and pepper. Stir well. Reduce heat to low and simmer until liquid thickens. Unless you want a pot of green mush **Do Not** overcook.
Serves 8.

Total Time: 40 mins.

Nutritional Values per serving

Calories 100, Total Carbohydrates 15g, Fiber 3g, Cholesterol 30mg, Sodium 90mg, Calcium 20mg, Protein 4g, Vitamin A 8%.

Denise's Succotash with Pazz

2 lbs fresh or frozen green lima beans
1 c water
1 can evaporated milk

1 16 oz can whole kernel corn, drained
1 16 oz can chopped tomatoes (optional)
½ stick butter

Thin flour paste mixture*
Seasoned salt to taste

Add green lima beans to boiling water. Cook until tender. Add milk, corn and tomatoes. Sprinkle seasoned salt and stir in butter. Simmer until butter is melted. Stir in flour mixture gently to desired thickness.
Serves 4

Total Time: 20 mins.

Nutritional Values per serving

Calories 100, Total Carbohydrates 15g, Fiber 3g, Cholesterol 30mg, Sodium 90mg, Calcium 20mg, Protein 4g, Vitamin A 8%.

French Fried Eggplant Stiks

1 medium purple eggplant
1 C olive oil or vegetable oil
1 T salt
Cold water to cover eggplant

Egg Batter
1 egg, beaten
½ C flour
dash seasoned salt
½ C water (add more water if necessary)

Peel and slice eggplant into thick rounds. Cut each round into three strips. Place in a bowl of cold water and salt. Heat oil in sauce pan or small deep fryer. Prepare egg batter. In small quantities place strips on a paper towel and pat dry. Coat strips with egg batter use tongs to lift into hot oil. Brown on both sides. Drain on a paper towel. Serve immediately.
Serves 4.

Total Time: 40 mins.

Nutritional Values per serving

Calories 542, Total Fat 57g, Cholesterol 36mg, Sodium 11mg, Total Carbohydrates 11g, Protein 1gm; Potassium 96mg, Fiber 2g, Iron 4%, Vitamin A 1%.

Zipping Hot Stuffed Grilled Eggplant

1 medium eggplant
1 lb thinly sliced ham or
1 lb seasoned ground beef*

oil
1 small jar salsa
1 8 oz container sour cream

Rinse and remove green hat on eggplant. Using a sharp knife cut out meat of eggplant. Be careful to leave at least ¼ inch of eggplant meat on sides. Set the center aside. Tightly stuff rolled ham into center of eggplant. Slice eggplant into several medium thick slices. Brush with oil and place on grill. Grill until eggplant is tender. No grill use frying pan. Brush top side with oil and turn over. Serve on small dollop of sour cream that has been mixed with salsa.
Serves 4.

*Seasoned ground beef mixture may be substituted for ham. Season and brown in butter center flesh of eggplant. Fry until soft. Serve hot.

Total Time: 30 mins.

Nutritional Values per serving

Calories 510, Total Fat 57g, Cholesterol 36mg, Sodium 11mg, Total Carbohydrates 11g,
Protein 1g; Potassium 96mg, Fiber 2g, Iron 4%, Vitamin A 1%.

Yellow Squash and Zucchini Combo

6 small yellow squash, unpeeled
3 small zucchini
¼ cup vegetable oil

1 medium onion
Seasoned salt and pepper to taste

Gently scrub squash with a soft brush or rub vigorously with your fingers. Cut off both ends of squash and zucchini. Now the old cutting board comes into play slice squash and zucchini into medium thick rounds. Slip them into a bowl of cold water as sliced. It's frying time again so pour oil in frying pan, heat on high. Shake off excess water and add handfuls of squash and zucchini to hot oil. Cover. Veggies will begin to sweat giving up their juices. Lower heat. Peel and cut onion into thin slices and throw in with the squash. Season lightly. Cook squash and onions until soft and most of the juice has been absorbed.   Serves 2.

Total Time: 30 mins.

Back in the day bacon grease was used instead of oil. Golly that is good and not so hard on the arteries if eaten only occasionally.

Nutritional Values per serving

Calories 240, Total Fat 28g, Cholesterol 0mg, Sodium 295mg, Calcium 40mg, Protein 2g, Iron 1%, Fiber 3g.

Derek's Baked Yellow Squash

3 medium yellow Squash   ½ C grated Parmesan cheese

Rinse squash and pat dry. Cut off ends. Slice each squash in half lengthwise. Place on cookie sheet. Sprinkle cheese on each half. Cover with foil and bake at 350° for 15-20 minutes until squash is soft.
Serves 4.

Total Time: 30 mins.

Nutritional Values per serving
Calories 300, Total Fat 12g, Cholesterol 36mg, Sodium 11mg, Total Carbohydrates 11g, Iron 1%.

Spectacular Batter Fried Squash Flowers

12 large squash flowers
1 C oil
Seasoned salt and pepper to taste

Egg Batter
1 egg
2 T flour
Enough water to make a thin batter

Squash flowers are delicate handle gently. Hold flowers by their ends and swish in cold water. Pat dry. Prepare egg batter. Heat oil in deep fryer or small sauce pan. Dip squash flowers in egg batter and carefully drop into hot oil cook until lightly browned. Drain on paper towels. Serve immediately.
Serves 2.

Total Time: 20 mins.

Nutritional Values per serving

Calories 340, Total Fat 27g, Cholesterol 36mg, Sodium 11mg, Total Carbohydrates 11g, Iron 1%.

Muriel's Spaghetti Squash Casserole

1 medium spaghetti squash,
   baked and raked
½ C Parmesan cheese
¼ stick butter (melted)

1 egg
½ C evaporated milk

Flip squash into a baking dish. In a small bowl beat the egg, milk, cheese and melted butter. Pour over squash. Combine thoroughly. Sprinkle additional Parmesan cheese on top. Bake at 350° until center is set.
Serves 2.

Total Time: 40 mins.

Nutritional Values per serving

Calories 243, Total Fat 16g, Cholesterol 132mg, Sodium 562mg, Protein 14g, Calcium 40mg, Potassium 84mg, Iron 1%, Vitamin C.

Winky's Mashed Rutabaga

1 medium rutabaga　　　　　　　3 C water
2 T butter

Peel and cut rutabaga into large cubes. Cook until very tender. Drain, mash and slather with butter.
Serves 2.

Total Time: 40 mins.

Nutritional Values per serving (Rutabaga)

Calories 340, Total Fat 1g, Cholesterol 36mg, Sodium 11mg, Total Carbohydrates 11g, Potassium 277mg, Calcium 40mg, Protein 1g, Fiber 1g, Sugars 5g.

Roasted Parsnips and Turnips

4 parsnips
3 medium turnips

1 T oil
1 package onion soup mix

Rinse and peel both veggies. Cut into bite sized chunks, slide into baking dish. Drizzle oil on veggies sprinkle on soup mix, coat completely. Roast uncovered at 350° until tender.
Serves 4.

Time Total: 20 mins.

Nutritional Values per serving (Parsnips and Turnips)
Calories 55, Total Fat 2g, Sodium 8mg, Fiber 2g, Sugars 3g, Protein 1g, Calcium 28mg, Potassium 286mg.

Good to the Last Kernel Corn Pudding

4 16 oz cans whole kernel corn, drained
4 eggs
1 can evaporated milk

1 C sugar
'Pinch of salt
1 stick butter. melted

Pour corn into a baking dish. In a bowl whisk together sugar, salt, condensed milk and butter. Pour over corn, mix well. Top with pats of butter. Bake at 350° until center is set. Serves 6.

Total time: About 30 mins.

Nutritional Values per serving

Calories 110, Total Fat 50mg, Sodium 8mg, Niacin 2mg, Vitamin B6 1mg, Vitamin C 7mg, Iron 2mg, Magnesium 37mg, Potassium 270mg.

Dorothy's Fried Corn

6 ears sweet corn
½ stick butter

½ C sugar
1 can evaporated milk

*Shuck corn. Be sure to remove all silk, bounce into cold water. Whip out a very sharp knife or corn kernel cutter on cutting board remove corn from each ear and scrape cob. Melt butter in frying pan. Dump in corn coat well. Add sugar and milk. Cook covered, stir frequently until milk thickens.
Serves 4.

Total Time: 1 hour

Nutritional Values per serving

Calories 110, Total Fat 50mg, Sodium 2mg, Niacin 2mg, Vitamin B6 1mg, Vitamin C 7mg, Iron 2mg, Magnesium 37mg, Potassium 270 mg.

Old South Corn Fritters

2 C pancake mix
1 can whole kernel corn, drained
½ stick butter, melted

¼ C sugar
1 T oil per pan of fritters

Prepare pancake mix according to box instructions. Add corn, sugar and melted butter to pancake mixture. In frying pan swirl oil cover bottom of pan. Spoon 2 cooking spoons full of batter into hot pan. Turn fritter when edges begin to brown. Remove from pan and slather with butter. Eat as is or with maple syrup. Serves 4.

Total Time: 20 mins.

Nutritional Values per serving

Calories 110, Total Fat 50mg, Sodium 12mg, Niacin 2mg, Vitamin B6 1mg, Vitamin C 7mg, Iron 2mg, Magnesium 37mg, Potassium 270mg.

Euronne's Sautéed Oychanshi* Mushroom Surprise

1 package each of Oyster, Chanterelle and Shiitake mushrooms (if loose, select at least 4 of each)
½ stick of butter

Carefully rinse mushrooms under cold running water. Forget about using a mushroom brush, your itsy bitsy fingers will do the job very well. Pat the babies dry with a paper towel. Shave off bottom tips of all mushrooms leave whole. In a sauté pan or small frying pan melt butter. Drop all of the mushrooms in the pan at once. Stir gently until most of the liquid from the mushrooms is absorbed. Remove from heat, cover until ready to serve.   Serves 4.

Total Time: 20 mins.

Nutritional Values per serving

Calories 100, Total Fat 11g, Cholesterol 30mg, Sodium 90mg, Fiber 1g, Potassium 84mg, Calcium 2mg, Protein 3g, Vitamin A 8%.

Robbie's Mushroom and Onion Delight

1 extra large Vidalia onion, thinly sliced
1 lb Shiitake mushrooms
1 lb Oyster mushrooms

6 Banana mushrooms
½ stick butter

Peel and thinly slice onion. Slice off thin piece of ends of shiitake and Oyster mushrooms rinse in cold water. Remove outer skin and rinse banana mushrooms, keep whole. Heat butter on medium heat until melted and foaming. Slide in onions. Reduce heat. Cook onions until translucent* and soft. Kick in the mushrooms and cover. Cook for 5 minutes. Stir occasionally. Set aside until ready to serve.
Serves 6.

Total Time: 20 mins.

Nutritional Values per serving

Calories 100, Total Fat 11g, Total Carbohydrates 9mg, Cholesterol 30mg, Sodium 90mg, Protein 2mg, Potassium 170g, Fiber 2mg, Vitamin C 10%, Iron 2% Calcium 2%.

Tia's Portobello Italiano

1 package of Portobello mushroom caps (at least three large caps),
3 cloves fresh garlic, minced
1 medium onion, rough chopped
3 stalks celery, rough chopped
¼ C vegetable oil or olive oil

1 32 oz jar spaghetti sauce
1 T Italian Seasonings
¼ C Parmesan cheese
1 C cooked rice or
1 small box cooked spaghetti

The mushrooms are a meat replacement. Sauté onions and celery in oil, cook until tender. Pull off mushroom stems, discard, rinse mushrooms under cold running water, pat dry. Chop mushrooms into bite size pieces add to celery and onions. Cook until mushrooms are soft. Pour in spaghetti sauce. Mix well. Add garlic and Italian seasoning. Simmer 10 minutes. Spoon mushroom sauce over prepared rice or spaghetti. Top with parmesan cheese. Serves 4.

Total Time: 45 mins.

Nutritional Values per serving

Calories 331, Total Fat 19, Cholesterol 15mg, Sodium 259mg, Total Carbohydrates 34g, Fiber 1g, Calcium 22%, Protein 8g, Fiber 1g, Potassium 406g, Iron 6%, Fiber 1g, Vitamin C 9%.

Portobello Burger Whiz

3 Portobello mushroom caps
Seasoned salt
1 large onion, thinly sliced
Lettuce of choice
3 Slices cheese

<u>Mustard sauce</u>
2 tsp mustard
2 tsp mayonnaise

3 Kaiser rolls
1 large tomato

Rinse mushrooms, pull of stem, pat dry. Sprinkle lightly with seasoned salt. Grill or sauté mushrooms in skillet until center is soft. Grill or toast rolls. Mix mustard sauce, spread on rolls. Layer lettuce leaf, tomato, mushroom, cheese and onion slice on rolls. Top with more lettuce. Serves 3.

Total time: 15 mins.

Nutritional Values per serving

Calories 331, Total Fat 19, Cholesterol 15mg, Sodium 259mg, Total Carbohydrates. 34g, Fiber 1g, Calcium 22%, Protein 8g, Fiber 1g, Potassium 406g, Iron 6%, Fiber 1g, Vitamin C 9%.

Silky Sweet Beets

1 bunch fresh beets (4-6)
½ stick butter

1 small can evaporated milk
Flour paste*

Rinse and discard beet tops and end pieces. Roll them on a cookie sheet or into a baking dish. Cover with foil bake at 350°. Remove from oven when tender. Stick a fork into top of beets and carefully rub off skin with a paper towel. Slice beets into medium thick circles. Splash milk into sauce pan, add butter. Simmer to low boil. Prepare flour paste. Whisk in flour paste a little at a time until slightly thicken. Add beets and sugar if needed. Most beets are sweet enough and do not require additional sugar. Serves 6.

Total Time: 45 mins.

Nutritional Values per serving

Calories 113, Total Fat 7g, Cholesterol 20mg, Sodium 64mg, Total Carbohydrates 12g, Calcium 18g, Iron 1%, Potassium 259mg, Protein 1g, Fiber 1g, Vitamin C 9%.

Roasted Beets

4 medium Beets   1 T oil

Rinse, peel and rub beets with oil. Roast uncovered at 350° until tender.
Serves 4.

Total Time: 25 mins

Nutritional Values per serving

Calories 113, Total Fat 7g, Cholesterol 20mg, Sodium 64mg, Total Carbohydrates 12g, Calcium 10g, Iron 1%, Potassium 259mg, Protein 1g, Fiber 1g, Vitamin C 9%.

Wacky Onion Beets

1 jar whole beets
1 container French Fried Onions
¼ C oil

<u>Egg Batter</u>
1 T flour
1 large egg, beaten
2 T water

Pour out beet juice. Dry beets thoroughly with paper towel. On cutting board cut beets into quarters. Prepare egg batter. In a plastic bag lightly crush onions. Heat oil on high. Dip beet quarters in egg batter shake off excess. Roll those babies in the onions, cover completely. Using tongs carefully drop beets into hot oil. Cook until desired brownness. Remove beets with slotted spoon drain on paper towel. Serve hot as side dish or stick a toothpick in each Wacky beet and serve at room temperature as an appetizer. Serves 4

Total Time: 20 mins.

Nutritional Values per serving

Calories 113, Total Fat 7g, Cholesterol 20mg, Sodium 64mg, Total Carbohydrates 12g, Calcium 13g, Iron 1%, Potassium 259mg, Protein 1g, Fiber 1g, Vitamin C 9%.

STARCH RECIPES

RICE

Some Kind of Good Rice

½ C each long grain and wild rice
½ C chopped roasted red peppers
1 rib chopped celery
1 small onion, rough chopped
1 tsp *grained mustard
2 C water

While rice is boiling add onions and celery. When rice mixture is done throw in roasted red peppers grained mustard for a savory flavor. Serve as side dish or stuff fish, pork chops or chicken. Serves 4

Total Time: 30 hrs.

Nutrition Values per servings

Calories 96, Total fat 0g, Cholesterol 0g, Sodium 8mg, Total Carbohydrates 22g, Fiber 1g, Calcium 8%, Iron 4% Phosphorus 87mg, Potassium 111mg, Vitamin B1 07mg, Vitamin B 20mg, Vitamin C 10%.

Baked Cheesy Rice and Onion Pie

1 C rice
2 C water
1 C sharp cheese, grated
1 beaten egg

1 C Bermuda onion, thinly sliced
1 chicken bouillon cube
1 small can evaporated milk

Boil rice with bouillon cube until tender. Slice onion. Grate cheese. Slip ¼ of rice in baking dish. Layer onion slices and cheese. Mix milk with beaten egg. Pour on milk. Layer until all ingredients are used ending with cheese. Bake at 400° until center sets and lightly browned. Serves 6.

Total Time: 40 mins.

Nutrition Values per servings

Calories 96, Total Fat 0g, Cholesterol 0g, Sodium 8mg,
Total Carbohydrates 22g, Fiber 1g, Calcium 8%, Iron 4%
Phosphorus 87mg, Potassium 111mg, Vitamin B1 7mg,
Vitamin B2 02mg, Vitamin C 10%.

Calvin's Dirty Rice and Tomato Casserole

1 C rice
1 C water for rice
1 tub chicken livers
1 chicken bouillon cube
1 medium onion, chopped
½ stick butter

2 cans Swanson's chicken broth
1 tsp basil
4 large eggs, beaten
1 tsp Thai chili paste
1 32 oz can hearty tomato soup
1 tsp sugar

Cook rice until tender. Meanwhile, rinse chicken livers. Throw livers, bouillon cube, onion, butter into large pot of chicken broth. When chicken livers are done grab them up and fling them onto the cutting board, wack into small pieces. Put those bad boys back in the pot flake rice on top. In medium bowl beat eggs, plop in Thai chili paste, soup and sugar pour over rice and chicken livers. Combine well. Pour into baking dish. Bake at 400° until center sets. Serves 4.

Total time: 45 mins.

Nutritional Values per serving

Calories 244, Total Fat 11g, Cholesterol 30mg, Sodium 101mg, Total Carbohydrates 33g, Fiber 1g, Vitamin A 8%, Calcium 2%, Iron 6%.

Good Ole Red Beans and Rice

1 lb small kidney bean
1 medium onion, rough chopped
3 stalks celery and leaves, rough chopped

Seasoning meat
1 package smoked sausage
2 C cooked rice

Rinse beans and begin cooking according to package directions. Add onion, celery and seasoning meat. Boil those babies until juice thickens. Add more water if necessary (beans should be soft, but not mushy) Remove seasoning meat 30 minutes before beans are done. Cut sausage into thin rounds. Scoot the sausage into the beans after removing seasoning meat. Simmer for 30 minutes. Ladle over cooked rice. Serves 6.

Total Time: 1 hr.

Nutritional Values per serving

Calories 350, Total Fat 11g, Cholesterol 30mg, Sodium 101mg, Total Carbohydrates 33g, Fiber 1g, Vitamin A 8%, Calcium 2%, Iron 6%.

Aunt Flo's Spinach and Bermuda Onion Risotto

1 lb box risotto
3 cans chicken or beef broth
1 stick butter
2 pkgs frozen chopped spinach

1 small Bermuda onion (red)
1 small clove garlic, minced
½ pint half and half

In large pan bring broth to a soft boil. Add risotto. Coat rice well, add garlic. Reduce heat to simmer. Stir occasionally. When broth is reduced by ½, squeeze out water and add spinach, butter and half and half. Continue cooking until risotto becomes soft, thick and saucy. Fold in chopped onion just before serving. Serves 6.

Total Time: 30 mins.

Nutritional Values per serving

Calories 181, Total Fat 19g, Cholesterol 53mg, Sodium 154mg, Total Carbohydrates 2g, Vitamin A 13%, Calcium 3%.

PASTA

Italian Veggie Pasta

1 box tri-colored pasta
1 16oz bottle Italian dressing
2 T butter
¼ C chopped sweet basil (optional)
1 medium onion, chopped

½ C chopped celery
1 can chopped tomatoes
2 T chili paste
Parmesan cheese

Cook and drain pasta. Combine all ingredients with cooled except cheese. Stir gently. Top with a generous portion of Parmesan cheese. Serve hot. If serving cold omit butter. Serves 6.

Total Time: 40 mins.

Nutritional Values per serving

Calories 57, Total Fat 3g, Cholesterol 10mg, Sodium 162mg, Total Carbohydrates 3g, Potassium 470mg, Fiber 1g, Protein 5g, Vitamin A 9%, Vitamin C 21%, Calcium 33%, Iron 1%.

Craig's Feel Good Linguini Alfredo

1 box linguini
1 can evaporated milk
1 C whole milk
1 stick butter

1 cup Parmesan cheese
1 T grated onion
½ C shredded white cheddar cheese
Flour paste*

Prepare linguini according to package directions. Strain and rinse linguini under cold water. Set aside. In linguini pot pop in both milks, butter and onion. Bring to a low boil. Stirring constantly drizzle in flour paste to make a thin sauce. Throw in cheeses, stir until melted. Add linguini, coat gently.
Serves 6.

Total Time: 30 mins

Nutritional Values per serving

Calories 57, Total Fat 3g, Cholesterol 10mg, Sodium 162mg,
Total Carbohydrates 3g, Potassium 470mg, Fiber 1g, Protein 5g,
Vitamin A 9%, Vitamin C 21%, Calcium 40%, Iron 1%.

World's Best Macaroni and Cheese

1 16 oz box elbow macaroni
½ C sharp cheddar cheese
½ C mild cheddar cheese
½ C Parmesan cheese
½ C Swiss cheese
*Wegman's black rind cheddar

1 can evaporated milk
3 C whole milk
1 stick butter
1 tsp season salt
*Flour paste
6 slices Mozzarella cheese, topping

Cook, rinse under cold running water and drain macaroni. Pour both milks into large pot. Bring to a simmer. Make flour paste and gradually add to the milk with a whisk until milk is slightly thickened. Add butter, seasoned salt and cheese(s). Stir until cheese is melted. Throw in macaroni, mix well, dump into baking dish. Top with Mozzarella cheese or more Parmesan cheese. Bake at 350° until bubbly. Serves 6.

Total Time: 45 mins.

*If using Wegman's black rind cheddar no other cheese is necessary. This is sauce is hearty and can be used for any recipe that call for cheese sauce.

Nutritional Values per serving

Calories 690, Total Fat 33g, Cholesterol 89mg, Sodium 620mg, Total Carbohydrates 5g, Fiber 8g, Sugars 6g, Protein 33g, Vitamin A 24%, Vitamin C 2%, Calcium 64%.

Grandpa's Spaghetti and Meat Sauce

1 16 oz box spaghetti
1 C celery, chopped
1 C onion, chopped
½ C minced carrots
1 medium green pepper, chopped
3 T Italian seasoning

4 cloves fresh garlic, chopped
1 32oz jar pasta sauce
2 lbs ground beef or turkey
2 T seasoned salt
½ tsp black pepper
2 T Thai chili paste

Cook spaghetti, celery onions, carrots and green pepper in a large pot. Brown meat in frying pan. When both are done throw meat, garlic, seasonings, Thai chili paste and pasta sauce into spaghetti pot. Simmer for 15 minutes on low heat, stirring occasionally. Serve with a sprinkling of Parmesan cheese and a large slice of garlic bread. Serves 6.

Total Time: 1 hr.

Instead of meat sauce throw in meatballs.

<u>Garlic bread</u>: Combine butter and homemade garlic paste. Spread on bread of your choice. Run under broiler until lightly browned. Serve hot.

Nutritional Values per serving

Calories 450, Total Fat 1g, Cholesterol 0mg, Sodium 237mg, Total Carbohydrates 7g, Fiber 2g, Protein 2g, Vitamin A 81%, Vitamin C 14%, Calcium 3%, Iron 2%.

Spaghetti and Parmesan Nests

1 box spaghetti, cooked and drained
1 C Parmesan cheese
1 large egg
1 T melted butter
½ C parsley, finely chopped

In large bowl beat egg, add cheese, parsley and melted butter. Mix well, set aside. Plop spaghetti into baking dish using a fork swirl spaghetti into individual nests. Spoon cheese mixture over spaghetti, top with more cheese. Bake at 350° until set. Serves 6.

Total Time: 30 mins.

> **Nutritional Values per serving**
>
> Calories 250, Total Fat 1g, Cholesterol 4mg, Sodium 237mg, Total Carbohydrates 7g, Fiber 2g, Protein 2g, Vitamin A 81%, Vitamin C 14%, Calcium 10%, Iron 2%.

NOODLES

Baked Egg Noodles

1 package Egg Noodles, cooked
1 large onion, finely chopped
1 can chicken stock

1 jar chicken gravy
1 C bread crumbs
2 cans water

Cook noodles in chicken stock, water and onion. When noodles are done throw in gravy. Mix well. Spread into baking dish. Top with bread crumbs and pats of butter. Bake at 350° until noodles are bubbly. Serves 6.

Total Time: 30 mins.

Nutritional Values per serving

Calories 250, Total Fat 2g, Cholesterol 4mg, Sodium 237mg, Total Carbohydrates 7g, Fiber 2g, Protein 2g, Vitamin A 81%, Vitamin C 14%, Calcium 10%, Iron 2%.

Noodle Veggie Soup

2 C each fresh broccoli flowerets, carrots, cabbage, tomatoes
1 pkg cooked egg noodles

4 bouillon cubes
6 C water
Seasonings to taste

Rinse veggies, peel carrots, thick shred cabbage, chop remainder of veggies into bite size pieces. In large pot pour in water, add bouillon cubes and veggies. Simmer until veggies are soft add noodles and seasonings. Serves 8.

Total Time: 30 mins.

Nutritional Values per serving

Calories 200, Total Fat 1g, Cholesterol 2mg, Sodium 237mg, Total Carbohydrates 7g, Fiber 2g, Protein 2g, Vitamin A 81%, Vitamin C 14%, Calcium 10%, Iron 2%.

POTATOES

Kick'n Potatoes au Gratin

2 lbs white potatoes, unpeeled
1 8oz package shredded
   sharp cheddar cheese
1 4oz package Three Cheeses
6 slices *Provolone cheese
1 can evaporated milk

½ C water
1 stick of butter
½ medium onion, grated
¼ tsp salt per layer
*Flour paste

Prepare cheese sauce while potatoes are cooking to fork tender. Simmer milk and water in a large saucepan, add butter and grated onion. Make flour paste*, whisk into hot milk. Whisk constantly to prevent lumps. Should lumps appear strain mixture and return it to the saucepan. Reduce heat. Do not let milk mixture get too thick. Small amounts of milk may be added to keep the sauce thin. Melt in all cheeses except Provolone. Stir constantly. Set aside.

Peel potatoes and slice into ¼ inch thick rounds. You can eyeball it. Layer potato slices in casserole dish. Sprinkle on salt. Cover with cheese sauce. Repeat process until all of the potatoes are used. Top with Provolone cheese. Bake at 350° until cheese becomes golden brown and bubbly. Serves 6.

Total Time: 50 mins.

* Swiss or American cheese slices may be substituted.

Nutritional Values per serving
Calories 250, Total Fat 23g, Total Carbohydrates 2g, Cholesterol 68mg, Sodium 3g, Protein 12g, Calcium 38%, Vitamin A 17%.

Southern Home Fries

2 lbs white potatoes
¼ C oil
1 medium onion, thinly sliced

½ small green bell pepper, thinly sliced (optional)
Salt and pepper to taste

Peel and cut potatoes into medium thick irregular slices. Throw them into a bowl of cold water to keep potatoes from turning dark. Heat oil. Shake excess water off potatoes and carefully drop handfuls of potatoes into hot oil. Cover. Cook on high heat for ten minutes.

Meanwhile, thinly slice the onion and green pepper. Reduce heat to medium high. Turn browning potatoes with a pancake spatula. Sprinkle on onions, green pepper slices, salt and pepper. Cover and continue frying. Every 5 minutes turn and mix potatoes until soft and mostly browned. Drain when lifting from oil. Dump into serving bowl. A great side dish for any meal. Serves 6.

Total Time: 40 mins.

Nutritional Values per serving

Calories 240, Total Fat 36g, Total Carbohydrates 2g, Cholesterol 110mg, Sodium 515mg, Protein 2g, Vitamin A 24%, Calcium 8%, Iron 2%.

Elegant Mashed Potatoes

4 large Russet potatoes
1 stick butter
½ cup heavy cream

1 small can evaporated milk
Salt to taste
enough water to cover potatoes

Baking potatoes make the very best mashed potatoes. Peel and cut potatoes into thick blocks, slide into boiling water. Cook until very soft. Drain. Plop potatoes into large bowl. Pitch in salt. Beat potatoes on high until smooth. Add small amounts of cream and milk until potatoes are thick and creamy. Whip, whip, whip. Serves 6.

Total Time: 40 mins.

Nutritional Values per serving

Calories 340, Total Fat 36g, Total Carbohydrates 3g, Cholesterol 110mg, Sodium 515mg, Sugars 3g, Protein 2g, Calcium 8%, Iron 2%, Vitamin A 24%.

Miz Margaret's Twice Baked Potatoes

1 large Russet or Idaho potato per person
1 T butter per potato
Salt to taste
heavy cream
1 small can evaporated milk

Rub oil on potatoes and bake on a cookie sheet at 350° until center of the potatoes are done. Remove from oven. Leave oven on. While hot, make a thin lengthwise slice down the center of the potato to remove top skin. Carefully scoop out potato into a bowl leaving a thin coating of potato all around to protect the skin.

Add butter and salt, beat on high. Gradually, add small amounts of cream and milk until potatoes are smooth but firm. Pile potato mixture into skins. Top with pats of butter. Bake until top is golden brown.

If you are in a creative mood, place ¼ of potato mixture in a pastry bag with a decorative tip and pipe onto top of filled potatoes. Picture perfect dish! Too much work? Take a fork and swirl it around on top of potato mixture; this makes a nice design too.

Total Time: 40 mins.

Nutritional Values per serving

Calories 170, Total Fat 18g, Total Carbohydrates 1g, Cholesterol 55mg, Sodium 257mg, Sugars 1g, Protein 1g, Calcium 4%, Iron 2%, Vitamin A 24%.

Come 'n Git 'em Roasted Red Potatoes

3 to 4 lbs large red potatoes, unpeeled
½ cup oil
1 pkg onion soup mix

Rinse potatoes pat dry with paper towel. Remove all blemishes. Cut into quarters. Throw in baking dish. Drizzle oil on potatoes, pop on onion soup mix. Toss potatoes until completely covered. Bake at 350° until potatoes are soft and lightly browned. Serves 8.

Total Time: 50 mins.

Nutritional Values per serving
Calories 120, Total Fat 14g, Total Carbohydrates 1g, Cholesterol 0g, Sodium 610mg, Protein 3g, Iron 2%, Vitamin A 20%

Rich and Sassy Cold Potato Soup
(Vichyssoise)

3 large all purpose white or Yukon Gold potatoes, peeled and diced
2 cans Swanson's chicken stock
2 medium leeks, thoroughly washed

2 T butter
1 C half and half
½ tsp white pepper (optional)
Garnish with fresh chives or thinly sliced green onion tops (optional)

Cook potatoes and leeks in chicken stock until tender. Pour leeks, potatoes and stock into blender or food processor. Add half and half, butter and pepper to taste. Cool to room temperature. Ladle into bowls. Garnish with chopped chives or green onion tops. For a change of pace this soup may be served hot. Serves 4.

Total Time: 40 mins.

Nutritional Values per serving

Calories 420, Total Fat 15g, Total Carbohydrates 26g, Cholesterol 53mg, Sodium 1,013mg, Protein 2g, Potassium 720mg, Vitamin A 5%, Vitamin C 45%, Iron 6%, Calcium 2%.

Simply Simple Fingerling Potatoes

2 lbs Fingerling potatoes
Enough water to cover potatoes

1 tsp salt
½ stick melted butter

Rinse potatoes. Remove any spots. Add salt to boiling water. Throw in potatoes. Cook until tender. Drain. Transfer potatoes to a serving bowl, drizzle in butter. Toss lightly. Serves 6.

Total Time: 35 mins.

Nutritional Values per serving

Calories 120, Total Calories from Fat 14g, Total Carbohydrates. 1g, Cholesterol 0g, Sodium 610mg, Protein 3g, Iron 2%, Vitamin A 20%.

Kel's Mouthwatering Sweet Potatoes

4 lbs Sweet Potatoes (not yams)**
2 sticks butter
Sprinkle on each layer of potatoes
4 T sugar
2 T molasses***

2 T pure vanilla
1 T cinnamon
1 T nutmeg
Thin slices of butter

** The word yams is sometimes interchanged with sweet potatoes. The difference: meat of yams is yellow, pasty and tasteless. Sweet potatoes are reddish orange inside and less starchy.

***Do not use blackstrap molasses, too strong.

Rinse and scoot potatoes into large pot. Boil covered until potatoes are fork tender. Overcooked potatoes will break up. Drain potatoes, cover with cold water. Peel, slice and layer potatoes one at a time into a large casserole dish. Cover with slices of butter. Sprinkle remaining ingredients in the order listed. Continue layering until all potatoes have been used. Bake uncovered at 350° until bubbly, approximately 15 minutes.

Molasses is the star ingredient of this recipe it enhances the flavor of the potatoes.

If you are feeling ambitious, try this old fashioned variation using the same ingredients: Peel and thick slice raw sweet potatoes. Throw sliced potatoes in large casserole dish. OMIT molasses. Add all other ingredients, coat potatoes well. Pour in a ¼ cup of water. Bake covered at 350°. This recipe requires that the potatoes be turned from the bottom up occasionally. Some will break up, no harm done.

Total Time: 1 ½ hrs.

Nutritional Values per serving

Calories 687, Total Calories from Fat 29g, Total Carbohydrates 100g, Cholesterol 80g, Sodium 320mg, Sugars 48g, Vitamin A 21%.

∽o∽

Connie's Fluffy Baked Sweet Potatoes

1 large sweet potato per person
1 T butter per potato
1 tsp melted butter per potato

¼ tsp nutmeg
1 tsp dark brown sugar

Bake potatoes on a cookie sheet until done. Thinly cut off the center skin of each potato lengthwise. Carefully scoop out potato flesh into a bowl. Do not break skin. Beat potatoes on high to remove lumps and any strings that accumulate on beaters. (If sweet potatoes are stringy, rinse beaters every few minutes to remove strings until all string are gone.) Add butter. Pile mixture into potato skins. Return potatoes to cookie sheet. Mix nutmeg and sugar in a small bowl. Splash melted butter on potato tops. Sprinkle sugar/nutmeg mixture on top of the potatoes. Bake at 450° for 10 minutes. Serve immediately.

Total Time: 40 mins.

Nutritional Values per serving

Calories 150, Calories from Fat 100g, Total Carbohydrates 26g, Cholesterol 25mg, Sodium 72mg, Sugars 1g, Protein 2g, Calcium 10%, Potassium 438mg.

Richard's Grits & Sausage Bake

2 C Grits, cooked
1 roll sausage, cooked
½ C sharp cheese, grated
½ C roasted red pepper, chopped**

Pour grits, sausage, cheese and peppers into baking dish. Mix well. Bake at 350° until center sets.

Total Time: 1hr.

**A jar of marinated, roasted red peppers works well in this recipe.

Nutritional Values per serving

Calories 181, Total Fat 19g, Cholesterol 53 mg, Sodium. 154 mgs, Protein 5gms, Total Carbohydrates 2g, Vitamin A 13%, Calcium 3%.

TELL ALL SECTION

Definitions applicable to recipes in this series of books.

Accoutrements – assorted embellishments (vegetables, leaves etc.)
Aerate – break up lumps with fork or whisk
Au Gratin – French for adding cheese to a dish
Blanching – to place in scalding water for a short time before freezing
C – cup(s)
Caramelized onions – cooked until golden brown
Celeriac – celery flavored
Complex carbohydrates – a combination of many starches and sugars
Dash – 1 small sprinkle
Dense meats – pork and beef
Diagonal – cut at an angle
Egg wash – one whole egg mixed with water and beaten thoroughly
Flour paste – flour and water mixture, use mini whisk or fork to combine
Gooey – sticky
Grained mustard – mustard contains some unground seeds
Irregular – in no particular order
Lycopene – one of several powerful antioxidants in fresh and processed Tomatoes
Mandolin – utensil used for slicing and dicing
Mealy – crumbly, little reduced flavor

Mortar and Pestle – mortar is a special bowl and pestle is the stick used to crush, grind and mainly pulverize herbs and spices.

Namby pamby – weak, bendable

Oychanshi – oy chan shi is a mixture of Oyster, Chanterelle and Shiitake mushrooms

Palate – roof of mouth that helps identify taste

Pinch – amount picked up between thumb and first two fingers

Render – fry until fat liquefies. Save rendered bacon for BLTs or breakfast

Root vegetables – vegetables grown in the soil only the stems and leaves visible

Rough chopped – cut into medium to large pieces

Sauté – fry quickly

Segue – continuation into next theme

Shuck – remove leaves attached to corn

Strip celery – remove top, bottom and any strings; save leaves for cooking

T – tablespoon(s)

Translucent – shiny, see through

Vegetable peeler – a utensil used to scrape carrots and other vegetables

Woody – tough stringy end of the asparagus stalk.

PREFERENCES

Butter v Margarine is a matter of personal choice. Both have non-lowering cholesterol ingredients although some margarines contain no trans fats. I have found that butter adds a flavor of unmatched elegance to any dish.

Seasoned Salt v Salt is a good practice. Why? Because seasoned salt has a lower percentage of salt with great flavor derived from other spices and herbs. Purchase several 16 oz jars of seasoned salt from Murry's stores for greater economy especially when on sale. Grey salt is a must for subtle flavor and lower salt content but can be pricey, Try Home Goods for the best price. Kosher salt has larger crystals than regular salt and should be used sparingly.

Salting Foods, in my opinion, potatoes, cabbage, eggs and fish require salt. When purchasing salt always check the label for the word *"Iodized"*. We need iodine in salt to help balance our thyroids. Enormous quantities of salt should never be ingested.

Breading mixtures usually contain salt, additional salt is not recommended. Jars of lemon pepper and citrus seasonings contain small amounts of salt they are good for reduced salt intake.

Salt in smoked turkey wings, smoked pork neckbones and ham bones usually make additional seasoning unnecessary.

Cost Effective Time and Money Savers include purchasing pure vanilla and specialty spices at Home Goods, Marshall's or similar stores. Cinnamon and nutmeg can be a bit pricy too, try Dollar stores.

A small food processor is invaluable as a time saving device.

Cooking Utensils purchased from Dollar stores are a good money saver and they have a very good selection. ***WARNING!*** Always examine these utensils thoroughly some are made of flimsy materials. Cooking tools that are rarely used should definitely be purchased at Dollar stores. Wait for TV cooking tools to appear in local stores. Saves a lot on shipping and handling fees and one of these products is usually enough.

REFERENCES

1. My First Garden Vegetable Dictionary by University of Illinois Extension and white rose.com
2. About.com: Home Cooking: Peggy Trowbridge Filippone
3. Gilroy Spice Company
4. Calorie King
5. Cook'n Recipe Organizer (Nutritional Calculations)
6. USDA Nutrient Data Base of Standard Reference, 1998
7. National Pasta Association

Made in the USA
Charleston, SC
20 October 2013